The Mysterious & Unknown

Mummies

by Adam Woog

ReferencePoint Press™

San Diego, CA

For Karen, my faithful companion in exploring the world of mummies

©2009 ReferencePoint Press, Inc.

For more information, contact:
ReferencePoint Press, Inc.
PO Box 27779
San Diego, CA 92198
www.ReferencePointPress.com

Picture credits:
Cover: Landov
AP Images: 6, 11, 21, 23, 26, 35, 54, 56, 63, 65, 68, 72, 81, 84, 87, 91, 93
Landov: 8, 32, 49, 77
Museum of Antiquities Basel/AP Images: 13
North Wind: 41, 43

Series design and book layout:
Amy Stirnkorb

LIBRARY OF CONGRESS CATALOGING-IN-PUBLICATION DATA

Woog, Adam, 1953-
Mummies / by Adam Woog.
    p. cm. -- (Mysterious & unknown series)
  Includes bibliographical references and index.

ISBN-13: 978-1-60152-054-8 (hardback)
ISBN-10: 1-60152-054-9 (hardback)
1. Mummies--Juvenile literature. I. Title.
GN293.W66 2008

393'.3--dc22   2007051466

CONTENTS

FOREWORD

"Strange is our situation here upon earth."
—*Albert Einstein*

S ince the beginning of recorded history, people have been perplexed, fascinated, and even terrified by events that defy explanation. While science has demystified many of these events, such as volcanic eruptions and lunar eclipses, some remain outside the scope of the provable. Do UFOs exist? Are people abducted by aliens? Can some people see into the future? These questions and many more continue to puzzle, intrigue, and confound despite the enormous advances of modern science and technology.

It is these questions, phenomena, and oddities that Reference-Point Press's *The Mysterious & Unknown* series is committed to exploring. Each volume examines historical and anecdotal evidence as well as the most recent theories surrounding the topic in debate. Fascinating primary source quotes from scientists, experts, and eyewitnesses as well as in-depth sidebars further inform the text. Full-color illustrations and photos add to each book's visual appeal. Finally, source notes, a bibliography, and a thorough index provide further reference and research support. Whether for research or the curious reader, *The Mysterious & Unknown* series is certain to satisfy those fascinated by the unexplained.

INTRODUCTION

Meet the Mummies

In 1922 a British archaeologist, Howard Carter, was searching for the tombs of ancient Egyptian royal mummies. It was frustrating work. Grave robbers had already spoiled most of the tombs, robbing them of treasure.

But then Carter found something amazing: the undisturbed tomb of King Tutankhamen. Along with the body of King Tut himself was spectacular treasure, including furniture, chariots, jewelry, and statues, undisturbed after more than 3,000 years. In the years since its discovery, this find has given the world an unparalleled understanding of life in ancient Egypt.

Tut and other Egyptian mummies are the most famous in the world—so famous that any preserved body is named in their honor. Arabic travelers who visited ancient Egypt saw mummies coated with black resin, which they thought was bitumen, a kind of sticky tar. In Arabic, the word for bitumen is *mummiya*. The English word *mummy* comes from this mistake.

Did You Know?

A mummy is basically a dead body that has at least some soft tissue (skin and, sometimes, hair, muscles, and internal organs) preserved long after death.

Many Kinds of Mummies

Although Egyptian mummies are the most famous, many others have been found throughout the world. Mummies have been found on every continent. These far-flung corpses are just as strange and fascinating as those of Egypt—often more so, because less is known about them.

All of them fall into two basic categories. Some were deliberately made mummies, such as King Tut. Others are accidental, such as mummies preserved in ice. Both fit the basic definition of a mummy: a body whose soft tissue (skin and, sometimes, hair, muscles, and internal organs) are preserved long after death.

Egyptian mummies were specially treated and then dried in that land's hot, dry deserts. But hot, dry conditions are not the only ones that form mummies. As a result preserved corpses turn up in some very unusual places.

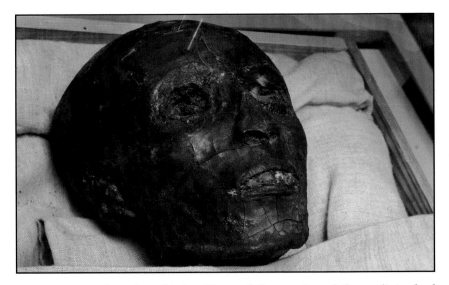

In 1922 a British archaeologist, Howard Carter, found the undisturbed tomb of King Tutankhamen. Seen here is Tut's mummified face.

Ghoulish, blackened bodies without bones emerge from the peat bogs of northern Europe. The preserved corpses of Roman Catholic saints have been on eerily lifelike display for hundreds of years. Inca children, sacrificed and left to freeze, have been found on nearly airless peaks in Peru. Explorers in the far north and ancient desert travelers have become mummies. And some Buddhist monks in Asia were so devoted to religious self-denial that they mummified themselves.

"Still Hanging Around"

Preserved bodies, natural or artificial, have fascinated people for thousands of years, partly because they are eerie—but also because they suggest an ancient question: Is there life after death? Mummies are about as close to immortality as humans can get, and it seems almost as though they hold the answer. Mummy experts Ron Beckett and Jerry Conlogue comment that mummies are, after all, the only ones we can ask about the afterlife: "Basically, they are the only dead folks still hanging around."[1]

In some times and places, mummies were objects of worship and respect. Egypt's mummies are a well-known example. Another is in Papua New Guinea, where some tribes smoke-cured their dead. After covering them in a layer of clay, the tribes placed the bodies on scaffolds that overlooked their villages and regularly visited them to ask for advice.

Such veneration still exists in some places. For example, thousands of people pay their respects every year to the permanently embalmed body of Soviet leader V.I. Lenin. And thousands of devout Roman Catholics pray every year before the earthly remains of "incorruptible" saints.

Even anonymous mummies can evoke strong feelings among

Mummified Animals

When people talk about mummies, they usually mean humans. Sometimes, though, animals are mummified as well. For example, the Egyptians often mummified cats, which they considered sacred. And the mummified remains of animals such as ancient woolly mammoths have been found in long-frozen parts of the world.

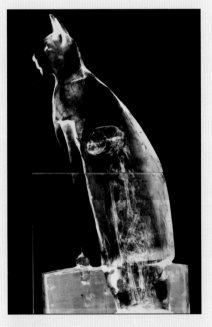

The Egyptians often mummified animals, including cats. Seen here through an X-ray is an Egyptian mummified cat.

the living. Science writer Heather Pringle comments: "Still recognizable as individuals, even after hundreds or thousands of years, mummies call to our imaginations. . . . We see each one of them as one of us."[2]

On a lighter note, mummies have also found their way into popular culture. Perhaps the most

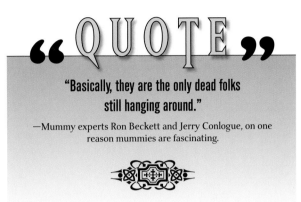

famous example of this is the 1932 horror movie *The Mummy,* starring Boris Karloff. It has been followed since by dozens of more films, books, and other media starring mummies.

Scientific Study

Perhaps the most important role that mummies play today is as the subjects of scientific study. Mummies, and the objects buried with them, teach the modern world a great deal about ancient times. The study of mummies reveals secrets about the history—and much more—of civilizations and periods long gone. Explorer and anthropologist Johan Reinhard writes, "A mummy is a magnet and can be used [to learn about] many subjects, including archaeology, geography, human biology, conservation, and the environment."[3]

Once, mummies had to be nearly destroyed in order to study them. However, new techniques such as X-rays, CAT scans, DNA analysis, and endoscopy (in which a tiny camera is inserted in the body) let researchers carry out their work while protecting the corpse itself. The mummies that have received the most thorough of these studies, in part because they are so plentiful, are those of ancient Egypt.

CHAPTER 1

The Most Famous Mummies of All

The first step to making a mummy in ancient Egypt was disembowelment—that is, removing the body's organs. This needed to be done as soon as possible after death. If not, the organs would become a breeding ground for bacteria and the body would rot.

Priests performed the mummification ritual, and their job was a sacred one. It was also difficult, requiring patience and careful attention to detail.

The job began with a cut on the left side of the abdomen to remove the lungs, stomach, liver, and intestines. These were stored in special jars, called canopic jars, one organ per jar. The jars were made of stone, bronze, pottery, or wood and usually decorated to honor the different gods who protect specific organs.

The first step to making a mummy in ancient Egypt was disembowelment—removing the body's organs. The organs were stored in special jars, called canopic jars, one organ per jar. This canopic jar held an organ of Queen Tiya.

There were two exceptions to saving the organs. One was the brain, which the Egyptians discarded because they believed it unimportant. They removed it by first breaking the bone between the eye sockets. Using a special tool (typically a hook or tube), they broke the brain into small pieces, then turned the body over and let the semiliquid organ pour out through the nose.

The other exception was the heart. The Egyptians believed that this organ was the source of thought and therefore very important. Journalist Carol Vogel notes, "While in ancient Egypt most of the [organs were] removed before a body was mummified, the heart was generally left intact."[4]

Treating the Body

The next step was to dry the body and coat it with oils and resins to preserve it. The embalmers also rinsed the body with wine, which helped kill bacteria. Then they packed it, inside and out, with a kind of salt called natron.

The salted corpse was left to dry on a table in a hot room for 40 days. By then the body was blackened and shriveled, but its joints were still flexible. The embalmers massaged the skin with more oils and perfumes to keep it flexible. The exact recipe for these treatments changed as various combinations were tried over time.

The priests next filled in the cavities where the brain and internal organs had been. They used clean natron and thick resin made from plants. This packing had two purposes: It maintained the body's shape and also preserved it.

Hairdressers and beauticians then made the face and hair as lifelike as possible. Sometimes they used an animal bone to prop up the nose and give it a normal shape. Protectors were placed over fingers and toes to prevent breakage.

To the Tomb

The embalmers then coated the body with another layer of resin and wrapped it in strips of linen—lots of them. A typical mummy needed about 150 yards (137m) of cloth.

As the linen was wound around the corpse, sacred charms such as amulets (jewelry thought to have magical powers) were placed in and around it. These were meant to protect the mummy from harm. Next the embalmers added an outer wrapping of canvas and a painted, decorated mask. Sometimes these masks were made of *cartonnage*, a kind of papier-mâché. More elaborate masks used gold, silver, and jewels.

When the body was finally ready, about 70 days after the start of the process, it was placed in a decorated, body-shaped container called a sarcophagus. The sarcophagus was carried, with great ritual, to a specially prepared tomb. Along with the body, the priests buried many useful or personal items, such as food, drink, pets, games, and musical instruments.

Why They Did It

The Egyptians developed their embalming and burial techniques over thousands of years. The details changed, but the basic framework remained essentially the same. Anthropologist

One of the final steps of mummification included adding a painted, decorated mask. Sometimes these masks were made of cartonnage, a kind of papier-mâché. More elaborate masks used gold, silver, and jewels. This mask was made for Tuyu.

Howard Reid comments, "The underlying principles guiding the mummifiers and the ritual timetable they adhered to seemed to change very little over the millennia."[5]

Mummification was done for one reason. The ancient Egyptians had a deep belief in the afterlife—in existence after death. In the afterlife, they believed, a person would live happily forever. But this person needed a physical body to have a successful afterlife. It was therefore crucial to preserve the corpse in as lifelike a state as possible, in a coffin painted to resemble the person.

It was also important that an elaborate funeral ceremony be held to reactivate the soul. At this ceremony, a priest prayed and performed special rituals, such as opening the mummy's mouth to symbolize breath returning. The priest also continued to make daily offerings at the tomb.

The Oldest Egyptian Mummy—All Natural

The Egyptians had an ideal climate for their death rituals and mummification. They simply added an embalming process to something that often occurred on its own. Even without embalming, the dry winds and hot sands of Egypt's deserts naturally worked to dry bodies by evaporating and wicking away moisture.

The oldest known Egyptian mummies were preserved in this natural way. The corpses were simply placed in shallow graves in the desert, away from inhabited areas near the banks of the Nile River.

The oldest of these mummies still in existence is a male, dating from about 3500 B.C. He is called Ginger because of his reddish hair, still visible even after more than 5,500 years. Ginger is so well preserved that even his fingernails can be seen.

Not much about Ginger's life is known, beyond that he was apparently a worker. He was found in a shallow grave with tools and some pottery (which once held food and drink for his journey to the afterlife). Probably, stones were once piled on top of Ginger's grave to keep animals away. After his discovery, Ginger was moved to the British Museum in London, England, and today he rests in a display that reproduces his ancient gravesite.

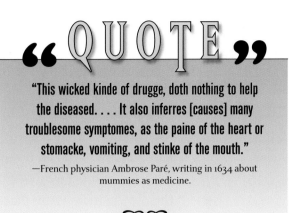

Seventy Million Mummies—or More

The Egyptians began experimenting with embalming around 3000 B.C. By about 2600 B.C. they had developed many of their techniques, such as disemboweling the corpses, and gradually they added other refinements. This required a lot of trial and error, experimenting with various substances and tools.

Inevitably, mistakes were made. For instance, embalmers tried burying bodies in clay jars, but this was unsuccessful because the jars trapped moisture and the bodies rotted. Egyptologist Bob Brier, an expert on mummies, writes, "There are many instances where the ancient Egyptian embalmer's art failed and the soft tissue crumbled, leaving only a skeleton."[6]

Making a mummy was time-consuming and expensive. At first it was a privilege reserved only for royalty. Over time, however, it also became available to other high levels of society. Egyptians who were wealthy but not royal considered mummification a status symbol.

By about 1550 B.C., every Egyptian who could afford the process arranged to be embalmed. This created a huge number of mummies over the years. No one knows exactly how many bodies in total the Egyptians preserved, but one estimate puts the figure at more than 70 million.

Mummies Lost

Mummification flourished in Egypt for about 3,000 years, but it faded away between the fourth and seventh century A.D. This is because many Egyptians became converts to Christianity, and the old customs were discouraged. Howard Reid comments, "In 394 AD, Rome officially adopted Christianity and, as Egypt was a part of its Empire, mass conversion . . . sounded the death-knell for the culture of ancient Egypt, bringing about an end to their traditional religion."[7]

Today only a tiny fraction of the millions of Egyptian mummies still exist. There are several reasons for this. One was the practice of grave robbing, in which thieves hunting for treasure wrecked countless tombs and destroyed what they considered worthless trash—the mummies they found in the tombs.

However, there were a number of other reasons as well. One was a craze that lasted for centuries, in both Europe and the Arab world, for making medicine out of mummies. Beginning in the Middle Ages, preserved corpses were routinely dug up and ground into a powder considered to have powerful healing powers. Ron Beckett and Jerry Conlogue note, "In the 1500s, it was part of every druggist's inventory, from the Middle East to Europe."[8]

Mummy the Cure-All

This medicine, called mummy or *mummia*, was said to cure practically anything. It was especially good, the Arabs believed, for broken limbs and cuts. But others used it to treat ailments

Journeying to Paradise

For the Egyptians, making sure a mummy could be recognized as an individual was very important. They believed a person's spirit left the body at death, but could be reunited later. Making the body as lifelike as possible and painting its coffin with a picture of the person helped the spirit recognize the correct tomb and return to the proper body.

This reunion was crucial for a proper afterlife. Science writer Heather Pringle notes, "To be reborn and to live forever in a land where everyone remained lithe and young and beautiful—surely a notion of paradise with universal appeal—a person's spiritual and life forces had to recognize his body and re-unite with it."

Heather Pringle, *The Mummy Congress: Science, Obsession, and the Everlasting Dead.* New York: Hyperion/Theia, 2001, p. 42.

ranging from abscesses, concussions, and paralysis to epilepsy, coughs, nausea, and ulcers. Even royalty used mummy as medicine.

According to legend, King Francis I of France, who reigned in the sixteenth century, always kept some handy, mixed with powdered rhubarb.

As the craze for mummy in Europe exploded, it was responsible for an increase in grave robbing, as dealers sought to get as much of it as possible. Mummy was in such high demand at some points that it was even faked. Unscrupulous dealers painted recently executed criminals with tarry pitch, dried them in the sun, and sold the results as genuine mummy.

Mummy remained popular as a cure-all well into the Renaissance. Even in the nineteenth century, it was considered an expensive, precious treasure. Bob Brier comments, "So prized was *mummia* that in 1809 the king of Persia sent the Queen of England a sample as a gift."[9]

The substance was popular even though it tasted horrible and its power was questionable. Not everyone believed in it. A prominent French physician, Ambrose Paré, wrote in 1634, "This wicked kinde of drugge, doth nothing to help the diseased. . . . It also inferres [causes] many troublesome symptoms, as the paine of the heart or stomacke, vomiting, and stinke of the mouth." [10]

Paint, Party Animals, and Fuel

Countless Egyptian mummies were also used in paint for fine artists. From the seventeenth century into the early twentieth century, the linen shrouds of mummies were highly prized as an ingredient in a certain shade of brown. The paint was called *caput mortum*, Latin for "dead head."

And yet another use for mummies—as entertainment—was found during the Victorian era of the nineteenth century. During this period in Europe, people were curious about far-away lands. It became fashionable for well-off people to bring mummies home from their Egyptian travels and hold "mummy parties."

These were public or semipublic events in which the mummies were unwrapped. Typically, lecturers explained the details of Egyptian mummy practices as the unwrapping took place. Sometimes admission fees were charged and brass bands provided further entertainment.

Archaeologist John H. Taylor writes, "Mummy 'unrollings' were often dramatic performances, carried out before fee-paying audiences drawn from the fashionable elements of European society."[11] They were considered both entertaining and educational. However, such gatherings also destroyed the mummies, since the bodies disintegrated once they were exposed to moist air.

Mummies may have been destroyed in still another way. According to a widespread legend made famous by Mark Twain, preserved corpses were so commonplace in Egypt that they were used as fuel on trains in place of wood or coal. This story has never been proven, and Twain himself made a cheerful disclaimer about the tale: "I am willing to believe it," he wrote. "I can believe anything."[12]

King Tut

Mummies in Egypt then were so prevalent that they were considered disposable. Even in the mid-1800s, when archaeologists and other scientists first started the field now known as Egyptology, the human remains they found were not as valuable as the treasures buried with them.

In 1857, for instance, when the first chief of the Egyptian Antiquities Service found the tomb of an important king, he saved the treasure and threw away the mummy. Today it is very different. Bob Brier remarks, "The Egyptian Supreme Council of Antiquities is so protective of the royal mummies that it is extremely reluctant to furnish even a single hair from the head of a pharaoh [king] for research purposes."[13]

Fortunately, not all of ancient Egypt's mummies have been destroyed. Many museums around the world have a mummy or two in their collections, and some have extensive and important holdings. The most significant collections of Egyptian mummies today are in the British Museum in London, England; the Ägyptisches Museum in Berlin, Germany; the Mummification Museum in Luxor, Egypt; and the Egyptian Museum in Cairo, Egypt.

The Cairo museum is home to, among other things, thousands of artifacts belonging to the world's most famous mummy, King Tutankhamen. Tut, the "boy king," was pharaoh from 1333 B.C., when he was about nine years old, until his death just nine years later. The cause of death is unclear; it may have been an infected broken leg.

In life, Tut was not especially important, but today he is world famous. This is because of British archaeologist Howard Carter's discovery of his burial site. It ranks as one of the greatest archaeological finds of modern times—and many would consider it the greatest.

The Mummy's Curse?

Carter's amazing discovery electrified the world's imagination and led to a worldwide fad for all things Egyptian. The opening of King Tut's tomb also created a long-lasting rumor that its discoverers were cursed. According to this rumor, a strange inscription was found above a door of the tomb that read: "Death comes

King Tut's body itself was not well preserved. Oils that were used on his skin had reacted badly to each other, partially destroying the body. Carter and his team partially dismembered the corpse as they worked. In the end, only Tut's head has survived intact. Here, Egypt's antiquities chief, Zahi Hawass, supervises the removal of Tut's mummy from its stone sarcophagus.

on wings to he who enters the tomb of a pharaoh."[14] According to the rumor (which has since proven quite false), several members of Carter's team died soon after the tomb was opened.

Besides the priceless collection of treasure Carter found buried in Tut's tomb was the body of the boy king himself. The royal mummy had been placed inside three coffins, the innermost richly decorated and made of solid gold. Tut's golden death mask, one of the most famous artifacts in the world, was part of this.

Unfortunately, Tut's body itself was not well preserved. Oils that were used on his skin had reacted badly to each other, partially destroying the body. Also, Carter, Tut's discoverer, was more interested in recovering the amulets tucked into the mummy's wrappings than the body itself. He and his team partially dismembered the corpse as they worked. In the end, only Tut's head has survived intact.

Magic and Mystery

Until recently, Egypt has fiercely protected the surviving part of its most famous mummy. Many of Tut's artifacts and his coffin have been displayed, and some have been exhibited around the world. But only a handful of people had ever seen the pharaoh's face between the time of Carter's discovery and the present. In the fall of 2007 this changed.

Tut's remains were moved to a climate-controlled glass display case in Cairo for public viewing. Only the head is visible; the rest of his body, damaged by Carter's team, is still wrapped in linen. Egypt's antiquities chief, Dr. Zahi Hawass, commented on the occasion of this viewing: "The face of the golden boy is amazing. It has magic and it has mystery. If you look at his face, you can feel the face of the golden king."[15]

King Tut is the best-known example of the most familiar mummies in the world—the mummies of Egypt. But these are by no means the only mummies in existence. This is because Egypt's desert is not the only good place in which to make mummies. Peat bogs, for instance, also work well, and in them the mysterious bog people of northern Europe were created.

In the fall of 2007 Tut's remains were moved to a climate-controlled glass display case in Cairo for public viewing. Only the head is visible; the rest of his body, damaged by Carter's team, is still wrapped in linen. The Egypt antiquities chief, Zahi Hawass, speaks to the press about the unveiling.

CHAPTER 2

Mummies from the Bogs

In 1983 some men working in a bog called Lindow Moss, near the town of Wilmslow in England, had a surprise. While digging in the earth, they discovered a severed head. It seemed to be partially mummified and not very old.

The workers had been cutting peat in the bog. Peat bogs are wetlands that are mostly masses of vegetation and water. The vegetation, called peat, becomes soft, tightly packed soil. Bogs are common in such northern European countries as Germany, Sweden, the Netherlands, Denmark, and the British Isles.

For thousands of years, people have cut peat out of bogs because, when dried, peat makes excellent fuel for fires and stoves. But peat bogs are also excellent environments for preserving bodies. A bog is fairly cold, with no oxygen and a high acid level in the water. All of these things prevent decay-causing bacteria from thriving, so a body trapped there will be preserved.

Ancient Mummy Solves Modern Murder

When they made their discovery, the peat cutters at Lindow Moss contacted the local police. At first the police thought that the severed head was evidence of a fairly recent murder. This mistake led to a strange outcome.

For over 20 years a local man named Peter Reyn-Bardt had been suspected of murdering his wife, Malika. While in prison for another crime, he had boasted of killing her, dismembering her, and burying the pieces in the bog. However, he later denied ever saying this. Since there was never any proof, he had never been arrested for her murder.

The first police report about the head indicated that the skull was that of a European female aged between 30 and 50. This description fit Reyn-Bardt's missing wife. When he was confronted with the news of the skull, Reyn-Bardt confessed to the murder.

It was only later, after scientists at Oxford University's Research Laboratory for Archaeology tested the skull, that it was found to be nearly 2,000 years old. The true age of Lindow Woman, as the head became known, was found before Reyn-Bardt was put on trial. He tried to take back his confession, but it was too late. He was sentenced to life in prison.

Lindow Man

In 1984, about a year after the discovery of Lindow Woman, workers in the same bog made an even more amazing discovery: an almost complete mummy. This time the peat cutters found a

"**Under the weight of overlying layers of peat, human bones bend, break, and warp until some corpses take on the grotesque look of melted toffee.**"

—Science writer Heather Pringle, on bog mummies.

Peat bogs, as well as bog mummies, are found all over the world, but especially in the northern European countries of Germany, Sweden, the Netherlands, Denmark, and the British Isles.

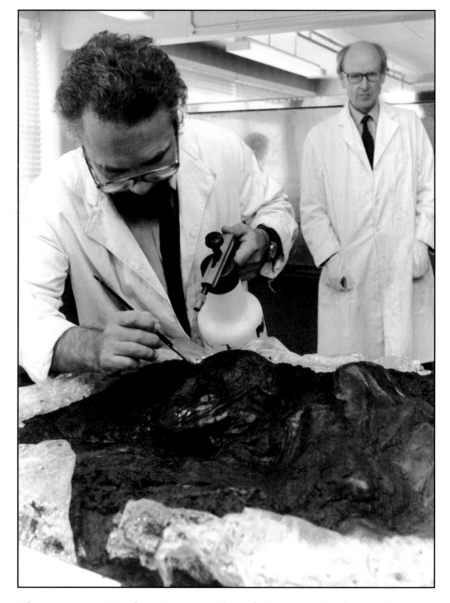

The mummy of Lindow Man, seen here being examined, was discovered in 1984 in a peat bog in England. Scientists believe he was in his twenties when he died, somewhere between 2 B.C. and A.D. 110.

head, torso, right foot, and arms. The arms were badly deteriorated, but the rest was remarkably well preserved.

This person, Lindow Man, was in his twenties when he died, somewhere between 2 B.C. and A.D. 119. At the time of his death, he was naked except for a fox-fur armband and a thong around his neck. He was about 5 feet 8 ¼ inches (1.7m) tall—probably a little taller than his contemporaries.

Lindow Man's skin has remained soft, like leather, and stained a dark brown by his years in the bog. His head is especially well preserved. His eyelids, eyelashes, and even eyebrows are clearly visible. So are his closely trimmed reddish hair and beard.

Four years after Lindow Man was discovered, more remains, including parts of two legs, were found in the same bog. Scientists think these pieces are more of Lindow Man, because everything combines to form a single, matching corpse.

The Bog People

The corpses in Lindow Moss are by no means the only bodies discovered in the bogs of Europe. Over the years, over 1,000 naturally preserved mummies have been recovered. Together, these corpses are called bog people or bog bodies.

Not all bog bodies are extremely old. Several date from just the last few hundred years. A few are even more recent, such as the corpse of a German soldier from World War II that was recovered in 1955.

However, like Lindow Man and Woman, most of the bog people died long ago—between 700 B.C. and A.D. 200. This period corresponds roughly with the time of European history called the Iron Age. During this period, people were just discovering methods for creating and using iron tools.

Did You Know?

Only around 1 percent of the original bog land in the western Netherlands still exists. The remaining areas are protected nature reserves. No new digging can take place there, so no new discoveries have been made.

Many bog bodies are remarkably well preserved. Even after thousands of years, they look like they died only recently. This is because the acidic and oxygen-free environment keeps them so well preserved that, in many cases, even their fingerprints can be determined. The police who investigated Lindow Woman can be excused for thinking they had found evidence of a recent murder.

On the other hand, bones do not usually survive in bogs. The acidity of the water softens them and makes it seem as if the mummies' skeletons have been removed. Heather Pringle comments, "Under the weight of overlying layers of peat, human bones bend, break, and warp until some corpses take on the grotesque look of melted toffee."[16]

Frequently, there is quite a bit of variation in how well bog people are preserved. In some mummies, for instance, individual internal organs can be easily recognized, while in others these organs decay. No one knows why some bog mummies are in better shape than others. Archaeologist Don Brothwell remarks, "The great variation in the degree of preservation of these bodies is very puzzling indeed."[17]

Violent Deaths

Lindow Man is typical in some ways of the bog people as a whole—for example, the dark brown, leathery quality of his skin. But Lindow Man has an even more striking characteristic shared by most of the other bog bodies. He did not die peacefully or by accident.

A handful of bog mummies died of disease or natural disaster. However, they are exceptions. Most of them met violent deaths at the hands of other people. Howard Reid states that the bog mummies "share one stark common characteristic: they all seem to have been deliberately put to death." [18]

In case after case, the bodies show evidence of murder, ritual sacrifice, or execution. The methods typically include fractured skulls, slit throats, or strangulation—and sometimes more than one method at once. This multiple-method murder is what happened to Lindow Man. Someone struck him three times on the head, slit his throat, and strangled him with a knotted cord.

No one knows who Lindow Man was or why he was killed. Perhaps he was a sacrifice, but he could also have been a convicted criminal or the victim of a robbery. His fingernails were smooth and neatly cut, indicating that he was not a laborer or warrior. And he had all but two of his teeth—evidence that he was generally healthy when he died. Was he a nobleman? Was he a priest?

Murder or Sacrifice?

Of course, evidence is not the same thing as proof. It is possible that the damage seen on bog bodies was caused by accident or nature. For example, a rope around the neck might be evidence of a desperate attempt to save a person from sinking. Also, some bog people have been found with their heads detached—but even this is not proof of murder, since neck muscles weaken after death and the head may have separated naturally.

Still, the case for deliberate killing is overwhelming. There are many theories about this. A number of experts suggest that people were killed and thrown into the bogs as sacrifices to powerful spirits, which ancient northern Europeans believed lived there. Evidence shows that a number died in the autumn, so they may have been offered to ensure good harvests.

"The bog claimed a life for a life, or, as some may prefer to think, the old gods took a modern man in place of the man from the past."

—Archaeologist P.V. Glob, on the death of a worker excavating Tollund Man.

Tacitus, a Roman historian of the first century A.D., supports the sacrifice theory. After visiting northern Europe, he recorded that some people there were killed and thrown in bogs as punishment for various crimes and that others were ritually sacrificed. Tacitus also mentions that slaves were drowned at the end of annual fertility ceremonies.

Another piece of evidence indicating murder is that several bog bodies have been found anchored down with wooden stakes. Don Brothwell comments that a body that has been staked down is "a somewhat eerie fact which may have had ritual significance . . . [but it] could equally well have been intended simply to ensure that the body did not float to the surface in a pool."[19]

In the case of Lindow Man (who is now in the British Museum), the contents of his stomach support the ritual-killing theory. His last meal was a vegetable and grain mixture that included mistletoe pollen. Mistletoe is poisonous, and it is unlikely the man would have eaten it willingly or by accident. Furthermore, the eerily peaceful expression on his face indicates that he may have died willingly.

A Modern Life for an Old One

Tollund Man, who lived during the fourth century B.C., was also discovered in a peat bog. Two brothers, the Højgårds, found him in 1950. They lived in a village called Tollund, on the Jutland Peninsula in Denmark.

The brothers were cutting peat near their home one day when they uncovered what was clearly a human face. Looking further, they found a body in a fetal (curled up) position. Howard Reid writes, "Removing a block nearly three metres [nine feet] below the surface, they suddenly found themselves staring at a face so perfectly preserved that they assumed he was a recent murder victim."[20]

The Højgårds notified the police, who quickly determined that the body had not died recently. The police also decided that removing it was a job for specialists. A team of archaeologists arrived to remove the corpse.

This team excavated a huge block, nearly a ton of peat, so that the body could be safely moved. No heavy equipment could be brought into the soupy bog. The huge block of peat had to be lifted by hand and placed on a horse-drawn cart.

It was such difficult work that one team member collapsed during the excavation with a fatal heart attack. P.V. Glob, the archaeologist leading the project, commented that, in a sense, this sadly evened the score: "The bog claimed a life for a life, or, as some may prefer to think, the old gods took a modern man in place of the man from the past."[21]

Killed!

A preliminary analysis of the ground around the body indicated that it and the body were thousands of years old. Later, radiocarbon dating of the mummy's hair placed his death more precisely, at about 350 B.C.

Further study revealed many more details about Tollund Man. He was naked except for a hide belt around his waist and a pointed leather cap. The cap was fastened tightly under his chin and almost completely hid his short hair. He was mostly clean shaven, except for some stubble on his chin and upper lip.

The scientists who inspected him also determined that Tollund Man was about 40 years old when he died. He was 5 feet 3 inches (1.6m) in height—fairly short, even for the time period in which

The corpses in Lindow Moss are by no means the only bodies discovered in the bogs of Europe. Over the years, over 1,000 naturally preserved mummies have been recovered. This bog in Germany hid a mummy until 2000.

20.06.2005
Gmk:Darlaten
Gem:Uchte
Kr. Nienburg
FST 5
MOORLEICHE

he lived (when people generally were shorter than today).

As with so many other mummies recovered from the bogs, Tollund Man had died violently. In his case, a noose made of two twisted leather thongs was drawn tightly around his throat and left clear marks on the skin under his chin and at the side of his neck.

The reasons for Tollund Man's death are still a mystery. However, as with many bog people, his internal organs were so well preserved that scientists could examine the contents of his stomach. This gave them a picture of his final meal—and a possible insight into his death.

A Ritual Death?

Tollund Man ate his last meal 12 to 24 hours before he died. It was a gruel made from vegetables, grains, and seeds, including barley, linseed, gold of pleasure (a kind of flax), knotweed, bristle grass, and chamomile.

In some ways, such meals were typical of Tollund Man's place and time. However, there were a few striking things about it. For one thing, it contained an unusually large number of different kinds of seeds and grains. Some grew wild and some were cultivated, and not all would have been easily available.

Because of this variety, some think that Tollund Man's last meal was a special one prepared just for him. This would bolster the theory that he was sacrificed. Speaking of Tollund Man and another mummy, Grauballe Man, Howard Reid comments, "The gruel they ate . . . contained so many wild herbs and grasses that some experts have suggested that these men were being prepared for death to ensure the fertility of the next agricultural season."[22]

Furthermore, the barley in Tollund Man's last meal contained ergot, a kind of fungus that can cause hallucinations when eaten. Perhaps, researchers suggest, whoever killed Tollund Man wanted to alter his mental state before he died. He may have been given this primitive drug prior to being sacrificed.

Tollund Man is now on display at the Silkeborg Museum in Denmark, near where he was found—that is, part of him is there: Only the head is original. Methods for conserving mummies were not as advanced in the early 1950s as now, and his body could not be saved. Visitors to the museum see his head attached to a replica of his body.

Yde Girl

Another remarkable bog mummy comes from the Bourtanger-moor region of the northern Netherlands. In 1897 peat cutters uncovered the remains of a body with red hair. The workers ran away in fright—they thought they were seeing the devil.

In fact, it was a girl of about 16 who died about 2,000 years ago. Yde Girl, as she was called, after a nearby village, was physically disabled. She suffered from curvature of the spine and was only about 4 ½ feet (1.37m) tall. One foot was swollen, suggesting that she walked with a limp. Her intestines contained blackberry seeds, indicating that she died in late summer or early autumn. One side of her head had been shaved.

She had been stabbed in the throat and strangled by a woolen belt wrapped around her neck, but no one knows why. Heather Pringle comments: "She may have been a slave captured from a neighboring tribe. She may have been a physical misfit selected as an offering because of her slight physical imperfection, a lopsided gait. Or it may be, as I choose to think, that she was simply an innocent child selected by village elders as the greatest gift [to the bog spirits] they could imagine."[23]

Yde Girl, named after a nearby village, was recovered in 1897 in a bog in the Netherlands. She had been murdered by strangulation; the woolen belt used was still around her neck.

Mummies in the Irish Bogs

I reland is another country rich in peat bogs, and hundreds of bodies have been discovered there. The most famous is Gallagh Man, who died at about age 25 sometime between 470 and 120 B.C. He was discovered in 1821 wearing a knee-length deerskin cape and lying on his side. Beneath the cape he had no clothes, although his clothing may have disintegrated. Two wooden stakes anchored him down, and around his neck was a band of willow rods that may have been used to strangle him.

Some of Ireland's bog mummies are more recent. For instance, Meenybraddan Woman was found in 1978. She was dressed in a cloak whose style is from the late sixteenth century. She apparently was in her late twenties or early thirties when she died, probably either a murder victim or a suicide.

"A Real Person"

Unfortunately, Yde Girl was not well treated even in death. The peat cutters who found her body hid it for over a week. Some local residents took souvenirs, pulling out her remaining hair and teeth. Eventually the local mayor arranged for her to be stored at the Drents Museum in the nearby city of Assen. Today this museum still houses her remains, part of one of the best bog-mummy collections in the world.

However, Yde Girl's body continued to be badly treated, and it has deteriorated. The mummy remained in obscurity until 1992, when a museum curator, Wijnand van der Sanden, commissioned a British forensics specialist, Richard Neave, to reconstruct Yde Girl's face. Neave made a CAT scan of her skull, then built a model using techniques from plastic surgery and other disciplines.

The result—a strawberry-blond beauty—captured the imagination of the public. This "humanized" Yde Girl became an international celebrity. People flocked to see her in the museum, and she was celebrated in books, radio plays, and poems. Van der Sanden notes, "People . . . can see now that she was a real person."[24]

The conditions that created Yde Girl and other bog people were vastly different from the dry deserts of Egypt. But mummies are created in still other places and environments around the world. Among them are crypts—those dark and mysterious stone vaults built beneath ancient churches.

CHAPTER 3

Mummies from the Crypts

In the far south of Italy is a sight not for the fainthearted: a collection of more than 8,000 mummies on public display. The corpses are organized by category, divided into men, women, virgins, children, priests, monks, and professionals. They are further arranged by age and social status.

Many of the mummies are elaborately clothed in the finest fashions available when they died—some from hundreds of years ago, some almost of the present day. Many are also carefully posed. Two children sit together in a rocking chair. Families are arranged as if at dinner. Military officers are seated as if posing for a group portrait. Women wear hoop skirts and carry parasols.

Some hang from the ceiling. Others lie on shelves or are propped up against walls. Oddly, there is no odor from all of these dead bodies. Photographer and writer Paolo Ventura notes, "The strangest aspect of all is that the assembled ranks . . . give off no smell at all, which is more than can be said for the living world from which they have departed."[25]

The Capuchin Catacombs Begin

This eerie place is the catacombs, or underground tunnels, beneath a monastery in Palermo. Palermo is the largest city in Sicily, the huge island off Italy's "toe." The monastery belongs to the Capuchins, an order of Roman Catholic monks.

The monks began their mummy collection out of necessity. When the cemetery in their monastery filled up in the late 1500s, the monks needed to find a solution to the space problem. They decided to embalm their dead and dig a catacomb beneath the monastery to house them.

The first person to be mummified there, in 1599, was named Brother Silvestro of Gubbio. According to some sources, his mummification was accidental. It happened when his body was temporarily placed in a dry well and Sicily's brutal heat dehydrated him.

Soon after that, the monks began perfecting their embalming process. It was complicated and painstaking. First they drained the bodies of liquid on racks of ceramic pipes, washed them with vinegar, and wrapped them in straw. Then they dried them in the hot Sicilian sun. By the nineteenth century, the monks had modified this method, adding a soak in arsenic or milk of magnesia to soften the mummies' skin.

Picnics with the Dead, for a Price

At first, mummification was a privilege reserved only for monks. Over time, however, the practice expanded. As in ancient Egypt, it became a status symbol for wealthy, important, or deeply religious townspeople to be embalmed. People donated generously to the monastery, with the understanding that they would be mummified after death. Sometimes they even specified what clothes they wanted to be wearing.

The relatives of these mummified people visited often. They prayed for the dead and made sure that the bodies of their loved ones were kept in good condition. Sometimes they even held picnics next to their departed relatives.

However, maintaining a relative in the catacombs was expensive. To keep family members there, people needed to keep contributing to the monastery. Otherwise, bodies were stored out of sight until the contributions resumed.

"High Ghoulishness"

The last monk to be mummified in Palermo was named Brother Riccardo; he was placed in the catacombs in 1871. Mummification was officially outlawed throughout Italy soon afterward. However, the wealthy citizens of Palermo kept requesting the practice, and the monks continued to oblige into the 1920s.

One of the last people to be entombed there was a two-year-old girl, Rosalia Lombardo. According to some sources, a relative embalmed Rosalia using a mysterious process, the details of which are lost. Whatever the process was, it apparently worked beautifully. Today, Rosalia remains strikingly well preserved in her glass-topped coffin.

She and the rest of the mummies in the catacombs are still on

N.° 1593. Palermo. Le Catacombe dei Cappuccini.

In the catacombs of Sicily is a collection of more than 8,000 mummies on public display. The corpses are organized by category. This nineteenth-century photograph shows hundreds of mummies lined up along walls.

public view daily. In fact, the catacombs of Palermo have become a major tourist attraction. It is a bizarre sight to modern eyes, but, for the monks who created the mummies, it was not only a practical solution but also an opportunity for serious religious contemplation. Historian Michael J. Lewis comments, "Here [is] high ghoulishness, of a sort requiring strong stomachs. But the ghoulishness had a distinct moral agenda [reason], intended both to demonstrate the monks' indifference to death and to steel them to it."[26]

"Here [is] high
ghoulishness, of
a sort requiring
strong stomachs."

—Historian Michael
J. Lewis, on the
Capuchin catacombs.

More Mummies in Churches

Many other European churches and cathedrals house mummies. For example, 18 are on display in glass cases behind the altar in the Church of the Dead in Urbania, Italy. These bodies, dating from the Middle Ages and Renaissance, were naturally mummified by a type of mold in their graves that dried them out. Among the mummies are a young Down syndrome victim, a woman who died during a cesarean birth, and a murder victim.

The basement of the church of Santo Stefano in Ferentillo, Italy, holds bodies similarly preserved by mold. Some still have clearly visible hair, beards, and teeth. Among them are a number of Chinese Catholics who died while on a pilgrimage route, as well as two birds mummified as an experiment by a doctor who hoped to find out more about embalming.

In Ireland, like Italy a strongly Catholic country, a number of churches also have their share of crypt mummies. The vault of Saint Michan's Church in Dublin, for instance, contains several corpses naturally preserved by the vault's dry, limestone walls. Among them are brothers Henry and John Sheares (hanged as the leaders of a 1798 rebellion) and a grisly, unidentified body missing its hands and feet.

According to legend, Saint Michan's is also home to a mummified veteran of the Crusades. However, this legend has proven to be false. Mummy experts Ron Beckett and Jerry Conlogue investigated the corpse and found a piece of fabric in its chest cavity. They had this carbon-dated along with some lung tissue and concluded, "The numbers that came back said he had lived two hundred years after the Crusades."[27]

The monks began their mummy collection out of necessity. When the cemetery in their monastery filled up in the late 1500s, the monks needed to find a solution to the space problem. They decided to embalm their dead and dig a catacomb beneath the monastery to house them. Pictured are two Capuchin monks in the catacombs.

Incorruptibility

Some of the most unusual preserved corpses in the world are those Roman Catholic saints known as incorruptibles. Catholicism

The first person to
be mummified by the
monks in Palermo
was named Brother
Silvestro of Gubbio.
He died in 1599. The
practice continued
until the 1920s.

teaches that the bodies of their holiest people, their saints, can be literally incorruptible—that is, they never decay. To pious Roman Catholics, the incorruptibles are preserved in miraculous and mysterious ways.

One famous example is Saint Zita, a thirteenth-century woman who in life was a lowly servant. Zita considered hard work to be a sign of devotion to God, and she refused to hate those who mistreated her. She became the patron saint of maids and domestic servants.

Like many incorruptibles, Zita's body is not only mysteriously preserved. It has also been known to give off a distinctive, sweet smell, known as the Odor of Sanctity. Her corpse, dark-skinned and dry, is today on display in a church in Lucca, Italy. Heather Pringle writes that she remains wonderfully lifelike: "Her gaunt face was smooth and her hands soft and supple-looking. Her lustrous nails gleamed. But for the dark color of her skin and the antique style of her dress, she looked as if she could have easily risen from her brocade bed and strolled the streets."[28]

Another well-known incorruptible is Saint Catherine Labouré. She was a nineteenth-century nun whose visions of the Virgin Mary led to the creation of a medal today worn by millions. After her death in 1876, Saint Catherine's body, with its lustrous blue eyes still visible, was put on display in a glass case in a small church in Paris, France.

In keeping with the common Catholic practice of dividing a saint's remains among several places, Saint Catherine's heart was removed and her hands amputated and replaced with wax replicas. Despite this, her body still seems lifelike. Anneli Rufus comments, "The flesh looks curiously fresh for having been dead since 1876. The corpse's eyes are open: Catherine's famous blue eyes."[29]

Examples of Faith

Since its earliest times, the Catholic Church has regarded incorruptible saints as powerful examples of faith. Portions of their bodies—sometimes just tiny fragments—are thus considered to be extremely holy relics. Heather Pringle writes, "Frail human flesh and bone [are] transmuted by the alchemy of faith into something holy and, as such, the remains of saints [possess] great powers for the good. . . . The bodies of saints, in other words, [are] divine lightning rods, capable of attracting miracles."[30]

Several other of the world's great religions have, over the centuries, similarly taught that the mortal remains of their holiest leaders will never rot. Writer Anneli Rufus comments, "The veneration [worship] of corpses, whole or dismembered, is arguably one of Western civilization's grisliest traditions. It is also one of the most enduring, transcending time as well as culture: bodily relics of Confucius, the Buddha, and Mohammed have been enshrined and adored through the millennia."[31]

Nonetheless, incorruptible holy people are primarily associated with the Roman Catholic Church. Not all of the Church's saints are preserved, and incorruptibility is not sufficient grounds by itself for canonization (the state of being declared a saint). Still, the Catholic Church does teach that the bodies of some saints are preserved through means that are unexplainable by science. Catholic writer Joan Carroll Cruz asserts, "The more carefully we consider the preservation of the incorruptibles, the more baffling does the subject become."[32]

Enshrined incorruptibles are found in Catholic churches, monasteries, and cathedrals all across Europe, particularly in Italy, France, and Spain. No one is sure exactly how many exist; estimates range from 100 to 300. Italian pathologist Ezio Fulcheri, an authority on the phenomenon, comments, "I don't think that any count is possible. Not even the bishops know how many there are."[33]

Saints Preserve Us!

Not all Catholic saints have been naturally preserved. Some were artificially embalmed. Some very early saints, for example, were embalmed using techniques quite similar to those of ancient Egypt. For example, records state that fourth-century Christians in Umbria, Italy, embalmed the body of Saint Emiliano with "aromatic resins and precious perfumes and white linens."[34]

Another example of an artificially embalmed saint is Saint Bernadine of Siena, Italy, who died in 1444. Joan Carroll Cruz notes about her:

> The body has been examined several times during the years, the last examination occurring in August 1968. The body at that time was found wrapped in tobacco leaves, and it was determined that preservatives had been used during a previous exhumation. Parts of the body are held together by various means, and chemicals were applied to the relic to maintain its condition.[35]

Embalming was frequently done to preserve a potential saint's body while he or she awaited canonization. This practice became so widespread that, in the eighteenth century, the Catholic Church was forced to regulate it. It decreed that only bodies that were soft, supple, and lifelike in color, with no disintegration and no artificial embalming, could be considered incorruptible.

The Self-Mummifying Monks of Japan

Far from the incorruptibles of Europe, in snowy northern Japan, is another unusual group of preserved religious bodies. Heather Pringle comments, "We are enchanted by the immortality that [mummies] represent. Even so, most of us shrink from the thought of actually becoming one ourselves."[36] And yet that is exactly what these Buddhist monks did. They mummified themselves on purpose.

These monks lived between the twelfth and nineteenth centuries. They belonged to the Shingon sect, a small group that combined classical elements of Buddhism with many other belief systems, including mountain worship, shamanism, Taoism, and magic. An important part of their religion was a belief in self-denial as a way to train the mind to ignore the physical world.

In an extreme example of this self-denial, some monks of the Shingon order mummified themselves. They saw it as a way to reach oneness with their deity, Buddha, and to demonstrate that the physical body is unimportant. They believed that only the most advanced religious masters could become such pure spirits that their dead bodies would not decay.

Two Thousand Days of Starvation

The process of self-mummification was rigorous and horribly painful. The monks slowly starved themselves by eating only a diet of salt, nuts, and seeds. At the same time, they meditated nonstop, surrounded by candles or burning peppers, which dried their skin out. They also subjected themselves to various physical hardships, such as extreme cold, so that their body fat was reduced to nearly zero.

This first part of the process went on for 1,000 days—almost three years. Then, for another 1,000 days, the monks allowed themselves to eat even less. They ate only a small amount of bark and roots from pine trees.

Toward the end of this period, they also drank a tea made from a tree sap that was usually used to make varnish. The tea made them vomit and sweat, drying them out even further, and killed any insects that might be likely to live in the soon-to-be-dead body. (In one monastery, the monks drank water from a sacred spring that contained arsenic, which killed bacteria in their bodies.)

As a monk neared death, other monks sealed him up in a small enclosure. Sometimes this was a dry pine box full of salt, sometimes an underground stone chamber, sometimes a room with a small air vent. In some cases, the monk rang a small bell each day to show that he was still alive. When the ringing stopped, other monks blocked up the air vent.

Mummified Monks Elsewhere in Asia

When the process was complete, the body was removed. In some cases, mummification failed and the body simply rotted. In this case, the corpse was resealed in its tomb. Those monks who had succeeded in making themselves mummies, however, were placed on display, dressed in fine robes, and revered by their followers. (According to tradition these mummies could never be touched by decay, but the monk's followers often further salted or smoked them anyway, just to make sure.)

No one is sure how many monks mummified themselves before the practice—which is, after all, a form of suicide—became illegal in the nineteenth century. Estimates of the number of mummies surviving today range between 16 and 24. Mummified monks are

Vu Khac Truong, a Zen Buddhist monk, died in the seventeenth century. His body was so well preserved that it has been restored and placed on display in a glass case in Vietnam.

The Mysterious Knight Kahlbutz

One mysterious mummy from the crypts is the Kahlbutz mummy. Christian Friedrich von Kahlbutz was a seventeenth-century nobleman in Prussia (now part of Germany). He was entombed inside his local church without any special embalming. However, the church was renovated in 1794, and several bodies, including his, were removed for reburial outdoors. All of them except the "Knight Kahlbutz" had decayed; he had become a mummy.

The Kahlbutz mummy has been extensively studied, but the exact reason for its preservation remains a mystery. Probably, the nobleman was naturally mummified through a combination of factors. These included extreme blood loss prior to death (he suffered from an unknown disease) and a well-sealed coffin that kept moisture out.

on display today at a number of temples in Yamagata Prefecture (state) and elsewhere.

But Japan is not the only place that has had examples of self-mummifying Buddhist monks. Similar cases have been detailed in several other Asian countries, including Vietnam, Thailand, Tibet, and Siberia (the far eastern portion of Russia). Apparently, this practice was once widespread and fairly common, especially in Tibet. It has been reported that hundreds, if not thousands, of mummified Tibetan monks were destroyed during the Chinese Cultural Revolution of the 1960s and 1970s.

One Tibetan monk who survived this period of destruction died around 1475 and was found in the 1990s. He had mummified himself through meditation, starvation, and slow suffocation. A belt connecting his neck and knees had forced him to maintain a lotus position, the cross-legged sitting posture used by Buddhists for meditation.

The self-mummifying Buddhist monks of Asia are unusual and fascinating. But Asia is home to other groups of mummies—including some of the strangest and most mystifying seen anywhere. Among them are the mummified people of China's forbidding Taklimakan Desert.

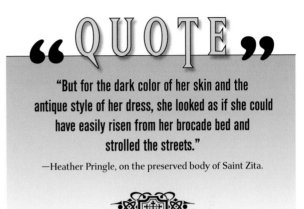

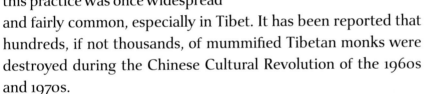

CHAPTER 4

Desert Mummies

In 1988 Dr. Victor Mair was in a small museum in the city of Ürümqi, in China's remote northwest. Mair, a professor of Chinese language and literature at the University of Pennsylvania, had been in the museum before. This time, though, he noticed something new.

Mair saw the entrance to a back room that had not previously been open to the public. He recalls: "It said something like 'Mummy Exhibition,' and I had the strangest kind of weird feeling because it was very dark and kind of cut off in the back part. There were curtains, I think. To get in, you felt like you were entering another world."[37]

The Tarim Mummies

The room was so badly lit that Mair needed a flashlight to get a good look at what was there. What he saw astonished him: Tall mummies with reddish-blond hair, fair skin, and brightly colored clothes. They were so beautifully preserved that Mair says, "I just couldn't believe my eyes, I mean, they looked as if they had died a few days ago."[38]

The professor had stumbled on the Tarim mummies, named after the area in which they were found. (They are also sometimes called the Ürümqi mummies.) Dr. Dolkun Kamberi, an archaeologist and a native of the Ürümqi region, had recently excavated them from tombs in the Taklimakan Desert. However, word of their existence had not yet reached the outside world.

The vast Taklimakan Desert, south of Ürümqi, is one of the driest places on earth. It has an annual average humidity of only 5 percent. It rains, on average, a mere 1.38 inches (3.5cm) annually. Furthermore, the land there is quite salty. This makes it a perfect environment for naturally preserving mummies.

Standing History on Its Head

The mummies Kamberi found in the desert date from about 1800 B.C. to A.D. 200. This does not make them the oldest mummies in the world. Nor is their manner of mummification unusual; they had simply been buried and naturally preserved in dry, salty soil. The most distinctive feature of these mummies is not even the fact that they are among the most lifelike found anywhere. An expert in ancient textiles, Elizabeth Wayland Barber, notes, "The famous mummies of Egypt appear dry and shriveled, blackened like discarded walnut husks, compared with these life-like remains."[39]

No, there is something even more startling about them: Their features are not Asian. Instead, they have strongly Caucasian (Western) looks. Their height, reddish blond hair, deep-set eyes, long noses and skulls, and full beards (for the men) are typical of the Celts of western Europe.

The vast Taklimakan Desert, south of Ürümqi, is one of the driest places on earth. Archaeologists have been exhuming mummies from the region since the late 1970s. Here, workers remove one of the mummies.

These physical features have created a puzzle for archaeologists and anthropologists. The region where the mummies were found was once part of an ancient trade route between China and Europe called the Silk Road. Most experts place the first opening of this trade route in the first century B.C. But many of the Tarim mummies date from a much earlier period than that.

How, then, did people with Western-looking features reach the remote deserts of China so long ago? And why were they there? When Victor Mair and his colleagues spread word of the mummies' existence, it shocked scientists around the world. The British newspaper the *Mail on Sunday* marveled that the discovery "stood history on its head."[40]

The mystery has yet to be solved. At the very least, the variety of tools and other goods found with the Tarim mummies (and other mummies all across the region) indicate that trade existed between Asia and Europe much earlier than previously thought. Elizabeth Wayland Barber notes, "Back and forth, to and fro. The passing of ideas between East and West clearly had a long history, and dry, sandy Central Asia served as the main corridor until quite recently."[41]

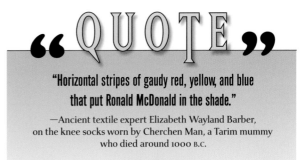

"Horizontal stripes of gaudy red, yellow, and blue that put Ronald McDonald in the shade."

—Ancient textile expert Elizabeth Wayland Barber, on the knee socks worn by Cherchen Man, a Tarim mummy who died around 1000 B.C.

Cherchen Man and His Family

The best known of the Tarim mummies, Cherchen Man, was about 55 years old when he died around 1000 B.C. In life, Cherchen Man was tall—some sources exaggerate his height at 6 feet

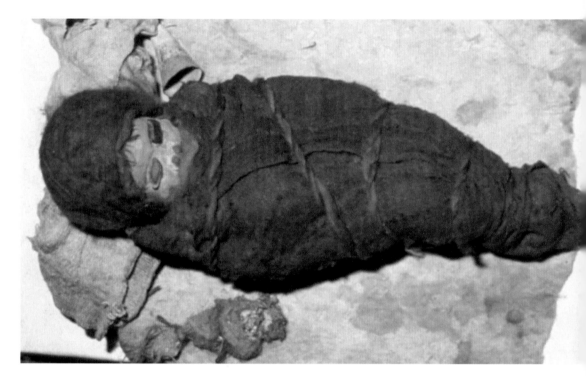

This mummified infant, about three months old when it died, was buried fully clothed, as were most of the mummies from the Tarim region.

6 inches (1.98m), though he was actually about 5 feet 9 inches (1.76m). He has red hair, a red beard, and a sun symbol tattooed on his left temple.

Cherchen Man was buried fully dressed, and his clothes were wonderfully preserved over the millennia. When he died he was wearing deerskin boots, a woolen tunic, and colorful knee socks with, in the words of Elizabeth Wayland Barber, "horizontal stripes of gaudy red, yellow, and blue that put Ronald McDonald in the shade."[42]

Two other bodies were buried with Cherchen Man, probably family members. One was a woman who stood about 5 feet 3 inches (1.6m) and had light brown hair and brilliantly colored clothes. The other was a one-year-old boy with blond-brown hair, a red and blue felt cap, and blue stones carefully placed over his eyes.

A cup made of a cow's horn and a nursing bottle made from a sheep's udder accompanied the baby. Someone had placed bits of red wool in his nose, perhaps to absorb moisture. Barber writes, "Time and the desert have so perfectly preserved the [baby's] face that its little ski-jump nose is intact, the tiny eyebrows still neatly arch above the blue eye-stones, and wisps of pale brown hair peek out onto the forehead from below the . . . bright blue bonnet."[43]

More from the Asian Deserts

Cherchen Man and his family are only 3 of at least 500 mummies unearthed in recent years in China's deserts. Victor Mair believes many more were destroyed or are still undiscovered. He writes, "Altogether we should probably be thinking in terms of at least several thousand mummies (not to mention tens of thousands of skeletons) that have already been uncovered in the Tarim Basin [alone]."[44]

One that has been unearthed is the so-called Beauty of Loulan. She died about 1800 B.C. and was found in A.D. 1980. This mummy has wonderfully preserved long brown hair, leather shoes, clothing, and a felt hat with a goose feather. Buried along with her were several items suggesting she was a farmer, including a bag of wheat and a tray used for winnowing (removing the husks from wheat).

This practice of burying people with items, similar to that of the Egyptian and other cultures, was common in China's desert regions. Among the items found have been tools for farming, carpentry, weaving, making pottery, raising animals, and making leather. Many hunting bows and arrows have also been found (but, curiously, almost no offensive weapons such as swords,

broadaxes, or armor). Howard Reid writes, "It certainly [is] not a problem for [modern] excavators to build up a detailed picture of how life must have been . . . all those years ago."[45]

Elsewhere in the Far East and Middle East, other desert regions have also produced mummies. Among them are several corpses, about 1,700 years old, found in an ancient salt mine in northwestern Iran. Other examples include the mummies of eight people in Lebanon who belonged to a religious sect, the Maronites, from the thirteenth century. These corpses, still dressed in beautiful clothes and jewelry, were found in a cave, where they apparently fled to avoid religious persecution.

The Oldest Artificial Mummies in the World

Asia and Egypt are not the only place with desert regions that can create mummies. On the western coast of South America is a narrow strip of land between the ocean and the fiercely dry Atacama Desert. This region is now part of Chile and Peru. It was home to an ancient fishing tribe called the Chinchorro, until they mysteriously disappeared about 1100 B.C.

The Chinchorro were not advanced in some ways. They had no technology for farming or for making pottery or textiles, and they had no written language. Nonetheless, they developed a complex system of ritual mummification. They started making mummies about 6000 B.C. This makes them the oldest artificial mummies in the world— far older even than those of Egypt.

The reasons why the Chinchorro developed embalming are not clear. However, it has been estimated that one in four of their tribe died before the age of one, and the majority of Chinchorro mummies are of children and unborn fetuses. (In fact, the earliest mummies are all children.) It has been suggested that grieving Chinchorro parents created mummies as a way to keep their dead children with them as long as possible.

Rebuilding the Dead

The Chinchorro literally disassembled and rebuilt their dead. First they removed the head, split the skull, and took out the brain. The other organs were then removed from the body. Skin and flesh were also carefully removed. Some experts have suggested that the Chinchorro may have ritually eaten some of the flesh of the dead person. However, there is no proof of this.

The exceptions to the skinning part of the process were the hands and feet. It was too difficult. Instead, the hands and feet were simply cut off and dried whole.

Next, the bare bones were dried, probably with hot ashes, and reassembled. The embalmers used small wooden sticks bound with reeds to give the skeleton strength, and fiber or feathers to pad it into a lifelike shape. The skull was filled with grass, ashes, soil, animal hair, or a mixture of these. A wig of human hair was added, attaching it with glue made from ash.

Over this framework, the skin was then painstakingly reapplied. If there were any gaps, skin from sea lions or pelicans was used. Next, the Chinchorro covered the body with thick layers of paint and paste made of ash, reattached the head to the body, and placed a painted, sculpted clay mask over the face. As a final step, they polished the outer paste covering with smooth pieces of wood or stone.

"They're Human Beings"

Unlike the Egyptians, the Chinchorro embalmers made no effort to mimic how individuals looked in life. Each mummy looked much like the other. Howard Reid writes: "The faces are elegant, almost serene, but lack individuality. The features are flattened and look like carefully designed masks. These are not images of how the person looked in life, but images of how the Chinchorro thought people should look after life."[46]

The Chinchorro left their dead in the desert, to be slowly covered up by shifting sands. The bodies were usually accompanied by a few possessions, such as a fishing line. Typically, family groups were placed together. But before this was done, evidence indicates, the Chinchorro kept the corpses for some time in their homes, perhaps displaying them at feasts and festivals.

The mummies thus remained part of the daily life of the people. To them, keeping the dead around was apparently normal. Anthropologist Bernardo Arriaza, an expert on the tribe, comments: "I'm still mesmerized by the care the Chinchorro put into reconstructing their bodies, because very often we tend to be shocked by the dead. We don't want to be around them. But it's hard to distance yourself from these mummies. They are not just archaeological artifacts, they're human beings."[47]

The Palomans

Perhaps the Chinchorro passed on their practice of mummification to other ancient South American tribes. For example, further north, between the Pacific coast and the Andes Mountains, a tribe called the Palomans began mummifying their dead around 4000 B.C. They salted and dried the bodies to preserve them, placing the bodies in sitting positions with their knees drawn up and hands clasped. They then wrapped the bodies in reeds and buried them under the floors of their homes.

Later, between about 750 B.C. and A.D. 100, another Peruvian

Buried Royalty

A mummy from the deserts of China called Marquise (Lady) Dai is one of the best-preserved corpses in the world. Buried in the Hunan region 2,100 years ago at the age of about 50, she was discovered in 1972. Her grave was a series of coffins beneath 5 tons (4.5t) of charcoal, which absorbed any water from the ground and kept her dry.

As a result, her joints are still flexible and her skin supple. Her internal organs are so well preserved that scientists could tell she had 138 melon seeds in her stomach. Further analysis shows she led a life of leisure and suffered from such ailments as gallstones and arteries clogged with plaque. It appears she died of a heart attack.

tribe, the Paracas, created hundreds of underground tomb chambers. Each chamber held roughly 40 mummies. Like the Palomans, the Paracas arranged these mummies sitting up, knees

Did You Know?

More than 100 corpses are on display in one of the world's only public museums dedicated to mummies: the Museo de las Momias (Public Museum of Mummified Citizens) in Guanajuato, Mexico.

pulled to chests. They then wrapped the mummies in layers of ornately woven textiles. Gold objects and mummified animals, such as parrots and foxes, were tucked into the layers of cloth. This made the mummy bundles very heavy, with each weighing as much as 330 pounds (150kg).

Over centuries, the Paracas developed mummification into a thriving system. Howard Reid writes: "By 400 BC the people of Paracas had developed an entire industry dedicated to preparing for the afterlife on a scale comparable to ancient Egypt. Thousands of human work-hours and huge quantities of raw materials were being consumed solely for the benefit of the dead."[48]

The Guanajuato Mummies

Further north in Latin America, still more examples of desert mummies can be found. One of the most spectacular is a group of more than 100 corpses in one of the world's only public museums dedicated to mummies. This is the Museo de las Momias (Public Museum of Mummified Citizens) in the Mexican town of Guanajuato, northwest of Mexico City.

The mummies of Guanajuato were victims of an epidemic of cholera—a highly infectious disease—in the mid-1800s. They were entombed in aboveground cement graves. According to legend, the citizens were so fearful of contagion that some of the sick people were buried while still alive. This is why the mummies have expressions of horror on their faces.

It is true that many mummies look like they died in terrible agony. However, they may well have died peacefully. After people die, their muscles contract, pulling their lips back and contorting them in other ways. As a result their faces typically have grimaces, and their bodies are twisted.

The mummies of Guanajuato were victims of an epidemic of cholera—a highly infectious disease—in the mid-1800s. According to legend, the citizens were so fearful of contagion that some of the sick people were buried while still alive. This might be why the mummies have expressions of horror on their faces.

A Tourist Attraction

Between 1896 and 1958 the bodies of these people were systematically removed from their aboveground graves. This was because of a local law requiring families to pay a tax on their relatives' graves.

Some families could not afford this. If the tax was not paid, the bodies were removed to make room for others.

When the bodies were removed, it was found that some had become naturally mummified. (Recently, evidence was found that a handful also received artificial embalming.) The exact causes behind the mummification are unknown. Some researchers have suggested that minerals in the ground may have been the reason. It also may be due to altitude and air quality. Guanajuato, in Mexico's central plateau, is over a mile high and usually dry.

In the early 1900s the Guanajuato cemetery workers began informally charging people to see the mummies they found. In 1969 a museum was created to formally house the best preserved of these bodies. Like the catacombs in Palermo, the museum is now a major tourist attraction.

Desert Mummies in the United States

The deserts found further north in the Americas, in the United States, have yielded only a few mummies. One, the oldest known human mummy in North America, was found in 1940 in Spirit Cave, Nevada. The mummy, a male about 45 years of age, died about 9,400 years ago.

This naturally preserved mummy was discovered lying on a fur blanket. He was dressed in a skin robe and leather moccasins, with mats wrapped around his head, shoulders, and lower body. Soft tissue has survived only on the head and right shoulder; the rest is just a skeleton. Dozens of tools and other artifacts were found along with the mummy, which is currently stored in the Nevada State Museum.

Also in the United States are mummies dating from more recent times—about A.D. 100. These were found in the ruins left by

the Anasazi, a tribe who lived in the Four Corners region of the Southwest. The tribe mysteriously vanished, and today little is known about it. The Anasazi mummies were found wrapped in fur and leather blankets and placed inside caves and rock holes. Many were wearing new, unused sandals, perhaps to help them walk to the next world.

The Anasazi mummies and the other mummies from desert climates were preserved because of intense heat and dry conditions. However, sometimes mummies are also created by the opposite conditions—the freezing temperatures of the coldest regions on earth.

This mummified infant is on display in the Guanajuato museum. It appears to be crying but no explanation for the expression has been given.

CHAPTER 5

Mummies
Out in the Cold

I n September 1991 Helmut and Erika Simon, amateur mountain climbers from Germany, were in the Ötzal Alps, near the
border where Austria and Italy meet, when they made a startling
discovery. They stumbled across a frozen body that had been
partially released from a melting glacier.

People often die in the rugged Ötzal Alps. Already that year,
six people had perished there. So the Simons were concerned
but not overly alarmed. The couple continued hiking and, when
they reached a mountain inn, contacted the local authorities.
These authorities retrieved the body by helicopter.

The corpse's identity was a mystery. No one had been reported missing recently. On the other hand, nothing at first indicated that the body had been there for a very long time. People speculated that it was perhaps 100 years old. The local newspaper stated: "The mortal remains of an unknown alpinist were discovered Thursday afternoon. . . . The identity of the corpse, which had been lying in the ice for several decades, could not at first be clarified."[49]

The 5,000-Year-Old Man

Soon, however, the story took an unexpected turn. The mountain police who removed the body took it to the Institute of Forensic Medicine at the University of Innsbruck, Austria, for further study. They also took a number of artifacts that were found nearby, including tools and scraps of clothing.

Closer examination revealed that the Simons had discovered something amazing. The body they found had been frozen in ice for thousands of years.

Forensic scientists made a rough estimate of how old the body was just by looking at the objects found with him. Among them was a distinctive ax with a copper head and a wooden handle, in a style used only during the early Bronze Age. One of the scientists, Konrad Spindler, said at the time, "An age of 2000 [years] before Christ, four thousand years ago, cannot be doubted in the least."[50]

Radiocarbon dating pinpointed the time of death more precisely. The ice man— for it was a man—had died sometime between 3350 and 3300 B.C. This meant he had been trapped in ice for well over 5,000 years. He was the world's oldest well-preserved mummy.

Ötzi

This 5,300-year-old mummy, known as Ötzi, was found in the Ötzal Alps, near the border where Austria and Italy meet.

One team examined the body while another returned to the site where he was found, hoping to find more objects. Further study of these revealed many details about Ötzi, as he was called.

He was mostly naked, but scraps of clothing still remaining indicated that he once wore a fur cap, a leather tunic, a knee-length cloak of woven grass, leggings, and shoes stuffed with grass.

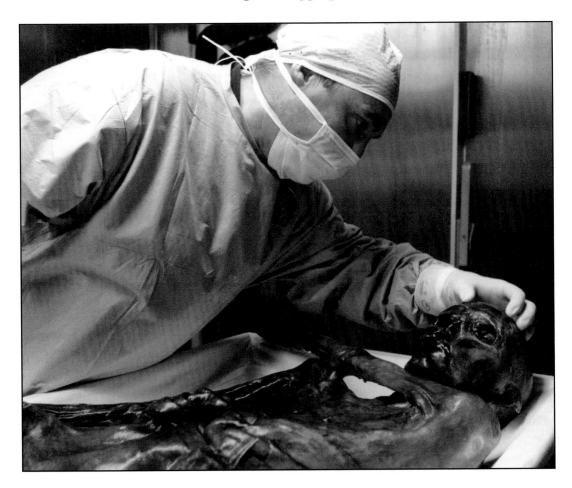

Furthermore, his leather backpack was still packed with a number of tools besides the ax, including a bow, arrows, and a sharp stone dagger. Ötzi had also carried a grass mat, two fire-making kits, and dried fungus (which was probably used as medicine).

There were other intriguing details. Most of Ötzi's hair had fallen out, but some was found on his clothes. It was still brown and wavy. He was tattooed in several places, including lines on his back, crosses behind a knee and an ankle, and stripes on the back of a leg. He was in his early to mid-forties when he died, and fairly small: about 5 feet 2 inches (1.6m) and 110 pounds (50kg).

Further analysis revealed that, in the last year of his life, Ötzi had suffered from arthritis, fleas, and parasitic worms. His tattoos were over areas where he had arthritis, suggesting they were made as a form of medicine. Ötzi also had black lungs, probably from years of breathing campfire smoke.

The Innsbruck scientists took great care to preserve Ötzi's body and his possessions. For example, he was kept in a special high-humidity chamber. It was maintained at 12°F (-6°C), the mean annual temperature of the region where he was found.

How Did He Die?

As details became known, an international debate developed over who should have possession of Ötzi. The body was in the care of the Austrian government. However, it had been found just inside Italy—to be precise, 303.69 feet (92.56m) across the border.

After a series of discussions, Italian authorities agreed to let the Austrians continue their study of Ötzi. Meanwhile, the Italian government began building him a permanent home. This

Ötzi's body was
discovered when it
was freed from the
ice by an unexpected
source: a series of
sandstorms in the
African desert that
sent huge clouds
of dust into the air
across Europe in
1991. Some landed
in Alpine glaciers,
melting the ice and
exposing the body.

state-of-the-art center, now open to the public, is the South Tyrol Museum of Archaeology in Bolzano, Italy.

Despite all the attention and study, many tantalizing questions still remain about Ötzi. One is the exact cause of his death. An arrowhead was embedded in his body, with a corresponding wound in his back. He probably died of internal bleeding from this injury. But why was he shot in the back? Was he fleeing from someone?

Furthermore, the arrow's shaft has never been found, leading to speculation that Ötzi may have had a companion who pulled it out. (His ribs were also broken, but it is unclear if this happened when he died or when he was dug from the ice.)

Another unanswered question is: Why was Ötzi so high up in treacherous country with relatively light equipment and few supplies? His bow and arrows were unfinished and unusable. Why would he have taken a dangerous journey without better weapons?

In any case, many experts believe, there was no ice when Ötzi died. They suggest that he was caught in an early blizzard, took shelter and died, and was trapped in the glacier later. Writer Brenda Fowler notes, "Virtually every researcher [accepts] the assumption that poor weather . . . forced the man to seek shelter in [a] trench, where he . . . died right on top of the boulder on which he was found."[51]

Juanita, the Ice Maiden

Far from the Alps, in the rugged Andes Mountains of South America, over 100 naturally preserved ice mummies have been found. The most famous of these is known as Juanita, the Ice Maiden.

She is amazingly well preserved, with long black hair, an elegant neck, and well-muscled arms.

Juanita was a member of the Inca, a mighty civilization that flourished from about A.D. 1100 to 1500. The Inca embalmed their royalty. Priests ceremonially clothed these corpses, parading them at important events and consulting them in times of trouble. But the Inca also practiced human sacrifice to mountain gods, and Juanita was one of these.

Very few Inca mummies (either royalty or sacrificial) survive today. The Spanish explorers who conquered the Inca in the 1500s destroyed as many mummies as they could (after stripping gold and other valuables from them). Looters later ruined many gravesites and stole whatever artifacts the Spanish had ignored. Nonetheless, a few mummies, like Juanita, were not found.

Sacrificed to the Gods

Juanita was about 14 when she died about 500 years ago, more than 20,000 feet (6km) up on Peru's Mount Ampato. The Inca believed that a sacrificed person would have a glorious afterlife, acting as a messenger between humans and their gods. The death was also considered good luck for everyone, journalist Christine Gorman writes: "Her sacrifice, considered the greatest honor her people could bestow, would appease the mountain god—the source of good fortune (in the form of rain to bless the crops) and terror (snowstorms, earthquakes and avalanches) to Inca culture."[52]

Sometimes sacrifices were buried alive, sometimes carried to mountaintops. In any case, the ritual was carried out with great ceremony. The children chosen were given beautiful clothing and

In the Andes Mountains of South America over 100 naturally preserved ice mummies have been found. The most famous of these is Juanita, the Ice Maiden (pictured). She is amazingly well preserved, with long black hair, an elegant neck, and well-muscled arms.

other valuable possessions. Writing in 1551, a Spaniard, Juan de Betanzos, noted, "Many boys and girls were sacrificed in pairs, being buried alive and well dressed and adorned with . . . items that [typically] a married Indian would possess."[53]

Because they were holy offerings, only the most physically beautiful young people were chosen. This purity made them acceptable to the gods. Bernabé Cobo, another Spaniard, commented in 1653, "These maidens . . . could not have any blemish or even a mole on their entire body."[54]

Killed and Abandoned

Juanita was found by two archaeologists: American Johan Reinhard and Peruvian Miguel Zárate. In 1995, while climbing Mount Ampato to look at a nearby active volcano, they discovered a "mummy bundle"—an Incan corpse wrapped in layers of cloth. Around it were gold and silver statues, food, and other offerings to the gods. Ash from the erupting volcano had melted enough ice to free the body.

Reinhard and Zárate cut a block of ice weighing about 90 pounds (40.8kg) around the body and carefully brought it down the mountain. Getting their treasure to civilization while keeping it frozen was difficult. They carried it by mule (with the body wrapped in sleeping pads to insulate it from the animal's body heat) and in the baggage hold of an overnight bus.

Juanita eventually arrived safely at the archaeology department of Catholic University in Arequipa, Peru. Study there and at Johns Hopkins University in the United States revealed much about her. For example, she was only about 4½ feet (1.4m) tall. She was slender and disease free, had good teeth, and had fasted for a day before dying.

An autopsy also revealed a fractured skull. This agrees with Spanish accounts, which indicate Inca sacrifices were often strangled or clubbed. Also, there were traces of corn liquor in Juanita's stomach. This was probably to make her sleepy before the execution.

"Her sacrifice, considered the greatest honor her people could bestow, would appease the mountain god."

—Journalist Christine Gorman, on Juanita.

Juanita was such a valuable find that *Time* magazine named her one of the world's top 10 discoveries of 1995. She is now in the archaeology museum of Arequipa's Catholic University. The mummy is kept safe in a glass box, maintained at a constant temperature and humidity to prevent decay.

The Tattooed Riders

Ötzi and Juanita were both frozen into accidental mummification. Some frozen mummies, however, were deliberately preserved—such as those of an ancient tribe called the Pazyryks. These hunters and herders lived in the Altay Mountains of southern Siberia. The Pazyryk mummies found so far date from 450 to 350 B.C.

One of the most remarkable is a woman of about 25 years of age. She was found in 1993 inside a log coffin, dressed in beige silk and a tall, 3-foot (1m) headdress with wooden birds sewn on it. Her blonde hair was still intact, although her brain had been removed through a hole in her skull and her other organs removed as well. The resulting cavities were filled with peat, bark, grasses, and herbs. Her eyes had been cut out and the sockets stuffed with fur.

The Pazyryks were excellent horse riders, and six horses were buried above this woman's grave, presumably for use in the afterlife. However, the animals' bodies decayed before freezing temperatures preserved them, so only their skeletons survived.

The Pazyryk mummies are notable for having the earliest examples found so far of complex, decorative tattooing. Among their tattoos are animals such as donkeys, rams, deer, and imaginary monsters. Howard Reid comments, "These tattoos are probably the most elaborate works of body-art to have survived from ancient times anywhere in the world."[55]

Burying and Preserving a Pazyryk King

We know about the mummification practices of tribes such as the Pazyryks through the writings of the Greek historian Herodotus, who visited them around 460 B.C. He wrote: "When a king dies they dig a great square pit, and, when it is ready they take up the corpse, which has previously been prepared in the following way: the belly is slit open, cleaned out, and filled with various aromatic substances . . . ; it is then sewn up again and the whole body coated over in wax."

The corpse was carried in a wagon from tribe to tribe before being laid in the tomb. Members of the king's household were strangled and buried with him, along with horses, gold utensils, and other objects. A year later another ceremony was held, in which 50 of the dead king's finest horses were killed and set upright in the ground around his tomb, and 50 of his most loyal subjects were strangled, gutted, impaled on poles, and set on the backs of the horses.

Quoted in Howard Reid, *In Search of the Immortals: Mummies, Death and the Afterlife.* New York: St. Martin's, 1999, p. 56.

Unlike the Inuit of Greenland, other Inuit groups artificially mummified their dead. For example, about 250 years ago the Inuit of the Aleutian Islands, off Alaska, embalmed bodies by removing the organs, stuffing the cavities with grass, drying them, and storing them in dry caves.

The Greenland Mummies

Another icy region, the far north of Canada, Greenland, and Alaska, is home to the Inuit people. It is also home to still more ice mummies. The most famous of these were found in 1972, when two brothers went hunting near an abandoned Inuit village on the west coast of Greenland, north of the Arctic Circle.

There they discovered eight mummies dating from about 1475—more than 500 years ago. The corpses had been buried and naturally mummified in the icy conditions. Typically, the Inuit of Greenland did not artificially preserve their dead, and most decayed normally. But in some cases—such as this one—caves or rock crevices protected them from direct sunlight, rain, and snow, keeping them both dry and frozen.

Six of the Greenland mummies were women between the ages of 18 and 50. The others were children—a 6-month-old baby and a 4-year-old boy. DNA analysis has shown that the 8 mummies belonged to 2 families.

Traveling to the Land of the Dead

Their last meals included seal, reindeer, Arctic hare, and ptarmigan (a type of grouse), typical food for the people of that region. Most of the women had tattoos on their faces, another traditional touch. Because the tattoos are faint and because the corpses' skin has darkened, they are visible only by infrared light.

It is unclear how these people died, or whether they died at the same time. However, analysis has shown that some were diseased. The four-year-old suffered from a serious hip disease, one woman had a great deal of soot in her lungs (probably from seal-blubber lamps), and another had throat cancer.

The eight were dressed in heavy clothing made from reindeer, seals, birds, and other animals. They were also surrounded by a number of tools and other objects. These were no doubt for their trip to the Land of the Dead, about which anthropologists Rolf Gilberg and Robert Petersen write, "Life in the Land of the Dead was very similar to life on earth except that there was no unsuccessful hunting or illness."[56]

The Franklin Expedition

Some frozen ice mummies date from more recent times. One of the most bizarre cases concerns the Franklin Expedition. This was a team of explorers led in the 1840s by Sir John Franklin of the British Royal Navy.

The Franklin Expedition was a team of explorers led in the 1840s by Sir John Franklin of the British Royal Navy. Franklin hoped to explore a section of the Northwest Passage in the Canadian Arctic. The team is thought to have accidentally poisoned themselves with lead. Years later a search team found their graves.

Franklin hoped to explore a section of the Northwest Passage in the Canadian Arctic. His was, however, an ill-fated journey. Bob Brier comments, "The expedition was equipped with the finest provisions and scientific equipment in the history of Arctic exploration, but none of the 129 men ever returned."[57]

Franklin's ships were trapped in ice over several winters in what is now Nunavut Territory. After three years with no word from the expedition, a huge, international search team was organized.

A number of clues were found. These included three graves and personal objects once belonging to crew members. Most telling was a message from April 1848, stating that many crew members had died and the survivors were heading south, dragging lifeboats behind them. Their frozen remains were found later. Some had been buried and had become mummified.

Death by Soldering

In the 1980s researchers looking for answers to the expedition's failure dug up several of these bodies. One was John Torrington, aged 20, buried on remote Beechey Island. The researchers had to cut through 6 feet (1.8m) of frozen ground to reach his coffin.

When Torrington was finally exposed, he had been naturally mummified. His teeth were clenched and his lips parted, and he was so thin that he had obviously been ill before he died. Nonetheless, the researchers reported, he looked almost peaceful.

The answer to the mystery of the Franklin Expedition was found when Torrington and the others were autopsied, and when cans of food left at the site were examined. The bodies contained extremely high levels of lead. Poorly soldered food cans had leaked this element into their rations.

Lead is highly toxic. It had weakened the men's health and left them vulnerable to pneumonia and other diseases. The lead also impaired the judgment of the survivors. Since they could not think rationally, when they set off across the ice they stocked up on useless supplies. The lifeboats they were dragging when they died were full of books, toothbrushes, soap, and other items worthless in terms of survival.

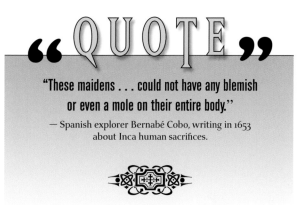

The Frozen Airman

An accidental ice mummy from more recent times is that of a military airman from World War II. In 1942 Leo Mustonen was aboard a plane that crashed during a blizzard 13,000 feet (4km) up in the Sierra Nevada of California. His body, preserved in glacial ice, was hidden until hikers spotted it in 2005. After Mustonen was identified, his body was returned to his hometown in Minnesota, more than 60 years after he died.

Leo Mustonen's death was an unusual case of a naturally preserved ice mummy from fairly recent times. More common today are scientific discoveries *about* mummies (both old and new). Breakthroughs in technology are creating amazing new possibilities for the preservation—and study—of these corpses.

Chapter 6

Thoroughly Modern Mummies

O ne area of mummy research in recent years has been in the field of permanently embalmed corpses. Most embalming today is temporary, meant only to last until funeral ceremonies are over. However, a handful of mummies have been permanently preserved.

The most famous of these is V.I. Lenin. Lenin was a revered leader of the Russian Revolution of 1917, which led to the creation of the Soviet Union. When Lenin died in 1924, several Soviet leaders proposed that his body be put on permanent display.

They wanted Lenin to be available so that future generations of Russians could pay their respects. Heather Pringle writes that one of those leaders, Josef Stalin, "envisioned perfection. He wanted a body that the Russian public could immediately

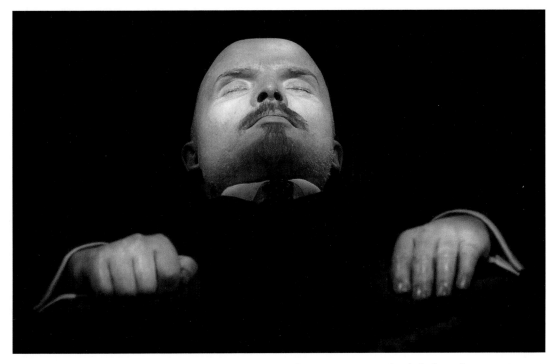

Lenin was a revered leader of the Russian Revolution of 1917, which led to the creation of the Soviet Union. When Lenin died in 1924, several Soviet leaders arranged for his body to be put on permanent display. It remains in Moscow's Red Square.

identify and worship, a body that was even more lifelike . . . than those of the saints."[58]

Preserving Lenin

A Russian doctor was assigned the task of embalming Lenin. Architects and sculptors created a suitably grand coffin and memorial building. Lenin was then put on exhibition in Moscow's Red Square. With typically dark humor, the Russian people coined an expression: "Yesterday, today, and tomorrow, Lenin is always with us."[59]

Except for a period during World War II when it was moved for safety, Lenin's body has been on display ever since. Tens of millions of people have lined up to see it over the years. On any given day a long line of viewers snakes out of the building.

Rumors that the body (now well over 100 years old) is not real, or that parts of it are fake, have circulated for years. These suggestions arise, in part, because of Lenin's strange, waxy appearance. The rumors are denied by Ilya Zbarsky, whose father helped perfect the embalming technique, and who himself became a member of the embalming team. Zbarsky comments, "There have been a lot of articles in the press saying that a hand was cut off or that just the head and the hands remain. They absolutely do not correspond to the truth; the body is whole and is preserved to this day."[60]

Lenin and Friends Stay Fresh

Lenin's body is still meticulously maintained. Twice weekly, experts open the glass coffin and apply embalming fluid to its exposed face and hands. In addition, every year and a half the corpse is immersed in chemicals, primarily glycerol and potassium acetate, that penetrate the skin and ensure that the body remains mostly liquid.

The Soviet success with preserving Lenin has inspired other Communist governments to do the same for their leaders. The bodies of Mao Tse-tung of China, Ho Chi Minh of Vietnam, and Kim Il Sung of North Korea have all been preserved and placed on public display.

The Chinese version nearly failed. When Mao died, the Chinese were not on good terms with the Soviets and did not ask for advice. They used far too much formaldehyde, and Mao's face became distended, with his ears sticking out and liquid dripping from his skin. Pringle writes, "Only hours of frantic salvage work . . . returned Mao to some semblance of himself."[61]

The body of still another former political leader, Philippines strongman Ferdinand Marcos, has also been permanently embalmed. Marcos's widow, Imelda, has refused to bury him until he is given a resting place in the national heroes' cemetery. Until then, Marcos remains in a refrigerated crypt in the town of Batac.

Evita

Another preserved political figure is Eva (Evita) Perón, the wife of Argentine leader Juan Perón. Evita was a powerful political force in her own right and loved by many Argentines, especially the working class and the downtrodden. Bob Brier notes that when she died in 1952, "she had become almost a religious icon to the poor of Argentina."[62]

At the public viewing of her body in Buenos Aires, Argentina's capital city, millions of mourners filed past to pay their respects. Juan Perón then planned a permanent display. He wanted to create a monument to his late wife larger than the Statue of Liberty, with her preserved corpse on display at the base. He asked a physician to permanently embalm her, a project that reputedly took a year and involved such techniques as paraffin injections and replacing the blood with glycerin.

However, fate took a strange twist. Perón was overthrown by a military coup in 1955, before he could build his wife's tomb. The new authorities removed all traces of the couple from public life. It became illegal in Argentina to have photos of the Peróns or even to mention their names.

"QUOTE"

"He wanted a body that the Russian public could immediately identify and worship, a body that was even more lifelike . . . than those of the saints."

—Heather Pringle, on Josef Stalin's wish to preserve Lenin's body.

Meanwhile, the new leaders hid Evita's body. In 1971 it was discovered that the body had been stored under a false name in a crypt in Milan, Italy. Following this revelation, the corpse was flown to Spain, where Juan Perón was living in exile. It remained in his house until 1973, when he returned to Argentina and was reelected president. Perón died soon after, and in 1974 the couple was buried together.

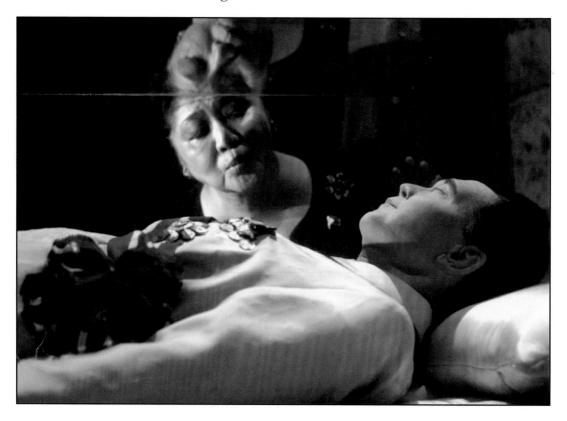

Philippines strongman Ferdinand Marcos has been permanently embalmed. Marcos's widow, Imelda, has refused to bury him until he is given a resting place in the national heroes' cemetery. Until then, Marcos remains in a refrigerated crypt in the town of Batac.

Bentham and the Auto-Icon

Political leaders are not the only ones to have their corpses preserved and publicly displayed. In the 1830s a famous British philosopher, Jeremy Bentham, wrote in his will that he wanted his body dissected by medical students. He also instructed that his head should be embalmed and his skeleton preserved. Then he wanted his skeleton filled out with straw, dressed in his usual clothes, seated on his favorite chair, and placed on display.

There are several possible explanations for Bentham's unusual request. Some people suggest that it was a practical joke. Others think that Bentham wanted to stimulate discussions about the spiritual implications of death. Still others simply feel that the philosopher thought dissecting his corpse and displaying what was left would help make death less mysterious and frightening.

In any case, the philosopher's wishes were carried out after his death in 1832 at the age of 84. As requested, Bentham's dressed skeleton was placed in a wood and glass cabinet he designed called the "Auto-Icon." It was then displayed at University College, London, which he had helped found.

Unfortunately, Bentham's head was damaged during the process. A wax replacement had to be made. Despite the grotesque appearance of the real head, it was also displayed for many years, resting at his feet.

Bentham's real head became the target of student pranks over the years (including being stolen several times), and it is now locked away. The body, with its false head, is still on display at University College. For the school's one hundreth and one hundred fiftieth anniversaries, it was brought to formal meetings of the College Council, which listed the philosopher as "present but not voting."

New Research

Scientific research on preserved human remains has progressed a long way since Bentham's days—and since the days when Egyptian corpses were carelessly unwrapped at "mummy parties." Today, scientists who study mummies do so with very sophisticated equipment and techniques. Among these are X-ray machines, CAT scanners, electron microscopes, and DNA analysis.

Unlike earlier methods, these do little or no damage to their subjects. For example, an endoscope allows researchers to examine the intestines and stomach of a mummy without cutting into it. Archaeologist John H. Taylor comments: "For many years, the only way to extract . . . data from Egyptian mummies was to unwrap them—a process both destructive and irreversible. Then, the advent of modern non-invasive imaging techniques . . . made it possible to look inside a mummy without disturbing the wrappings in any way."[63]

New technology does not work well in all cases. For example, X-rays are not effective tools for examining bog bodies, because skeletons typically dissolve in bogs and leave only flesh and organs. However, other methods can usually be used. A process called xeroradiography, for instance, was used to prove that Lindow Man had suffered serious skull fractures from a blunt weapon.

Studying Old Bodies

Such analysis continues to provide valuable information about the lifestyles, professions, relationships, health, diseases, injuries, and diets of ancient people. Bob Brier comments, "By studying mummies, we can learn about a disease in the ancient world that may help us cure a disease in the modern world. We can predict its course and perhaps be able to figure out a cure. Studying ancient malaria, for example, can help us find out more about what's happening with modern malaria and possibly find a cure."[64]

Even drug use in ancient corpses can be examined, and such research may shed light on a much wider issue—possible contact between groups of ancient people. A German toxicologist, Svetlana Balabanova, claims to have found traces of cocaine, marijuana, and tobacco in Egyptian mummies.

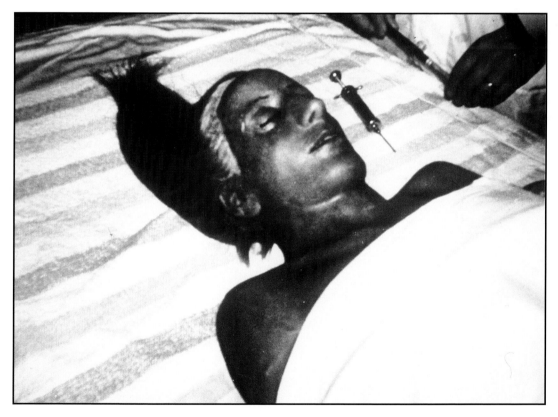

Eva (Evita) Perón, the wife of Argentine leader Juan Perón, was permanently preserved by order of her husband. The project reputedly took a year and involved such techniques as paraffin injections and replacing the blood with glycerin. Her body was later buried alongside her husband.

The Strange Saga of the Bank-Robber Mummy

In 1976 a mummy popped up in a very unexpected place. An episode of the television show *The Six Million Dollar Man* was being filmed at a house of horrors in an amusement park in Long Beach, California. The TV crew wanted to move what they thought was a fake mummy—but its arm fell off, exposing bone. It was a real mummy.

The corpse was Elmer McCurdy, an Oklahoma train robber who was killed while trying to escape capture in 1911. His body had been taken to a local funeral home and preserved with arsenic. No one claimed the body, so the undertaker charged the public a nickel to see the body. McCurdy's remains were then shown in a circus sideshow for years before landing in the California house of horrors. He was finally buried in Oklahoma.

If her controversial findings are accurate, it is evidence that the Egyptians had direct contact with the people of South America (where these substances originated) 1,600 years or more before

Columbus. This date is far earlier for contact between the hemispheres than is generally acknowledged.

Changes in Attitude

The ways in which ancient mummies are being studied today do not only concern the equipment used. Another important change has been in the way archaeologists and others treat mummies and the artifacts that are found with them.

Researchers now tend to be much more sensitive toward mummies as human beings, not just as objects of study. In the words of one Chilean archaeologist, "Mummies were actual people. They lived their lives, they died, they suffered, they ate, they made love, as people do today. . . . We are dealing with human beings and not with samples."[65]

This increased sensitivity has been supported by increasingly strict laws about digging up ancient graves, especially in North America. For example, Native American tribes now have much more of a voice than before in deciding what happens to their ancient artifacts.

This shift has had both positive and negative effects on the study of mummies. Stronger laws rightfully protect the human rights of the corpses. However, these laws also hinder scientific study that could benefit the living. Heather Pringle comments, "This [change] righted some wrongs, but . . . left an unfortunate scientific legacy: the study of North America's ancient dead [has] become virtually taboo."[66]

"Don't Try This at Home, Kids"

One group of scientists made an experiment about ancient Egyptian mummies that did not involve an actual ancient mummy. In

A famous
philosopher, Jeremy
Bentham, ordered in
his will that his body
be partially mum-
mified and placed
on display after his
death in 1832. It is
still available for
viewing at University
College, London.

1994 Dr. Bob Brier, an Egyptologist at Long Island University, and Ronald Wade, the director of the Maryland State Anatomy Board, led the project. Their team successfully created a mummy using ancient Egyptian methods—to their knowledge, the first time this had been done in thousands of years.

As closely as possible, the team re-created ancient Egyptian rituals and used replicas of their tools. For example, they used flint knives to cut the body and used special clay jars to store the organs. Brier estimates that it took about 10 years of research before the actual experiment began. He comments, "We had to do a lot of research, including looking at the temple walls and reading ancient sources. But the really hard part was putting the team together; we had to have ceramics people make the vases for us and we had to find ancient surgical tools. . . . Don't try this at home, kids—we're all professionals. We may not get paid, but we're all professionals!"[67]

Embalm Like an Egyptian

Their subject was the cadaver of a 76-year-old man that had its organs removed but underwent no other form of embalming. Once the corpse was disemboweled, it was covered and packed with natron—a lot of it. The team needed more than 550 pounds (249kg) of the salt, specially imported from Egypt. Then they put the body in a storeroom maintained at 104°F (40°C) to simulate an average Egyptian summer day. The body remained there for five weeks. When the researchers opened the room and removed the natron crust, they noticed no smell except for a faint peppery odor. The body weighed half of its initial 150 pounds (68kg). Furthermore, the corpse looked different. Brier writes that it "had the appearance of an ancient Egyptian mummy. The hands and

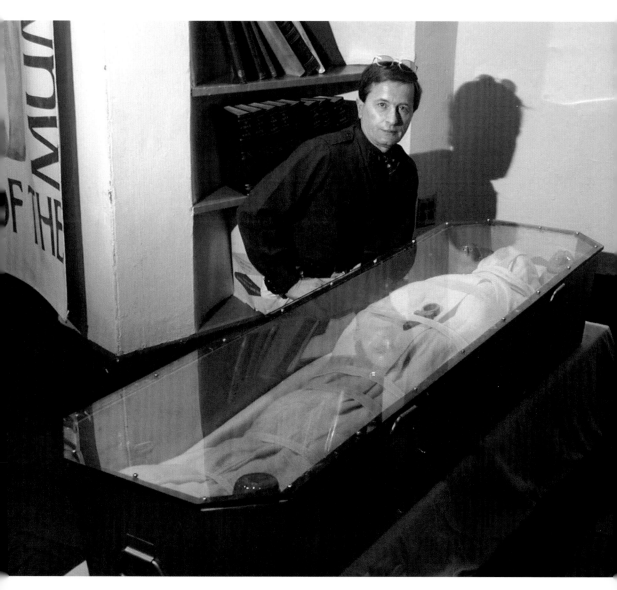

One group of scientists conducted an experiment about ancient Egyptian mummies that did not involve an actual ancient mummy. In 1994, a team including Ronald Wade, the director of the Maryland State Anatomy Board, led the project. Pictured are Wade and the mummy.

feet were dark and hard to the touch."[68]

The team then anointed the body with oils and wrapped it in linen, as the ancient Egyptians would have done. Then it left the corpse in the temperature-controlled room again, this time for five months. The result was a mummy that was, in virtually all respects, exactly like one from ancient Egypt.

Making a Modern Mummy

Not all modern scientists who are interested in permanent embalming want to faithfully re-create the Egyptian process. Several other techniques are currently being developed as well.

One well-known but controversial (and still unproven) method is cryonics, an experimental procedure of deep-freezing bodies. Typically, its purpose is to freeze and preserve bodies that are terminally ill or otherwise cannot be kept alive by today's science. The hope is that doctors will someday be able to revive and cure them.

Still another modern technique for preserving bodies—but not in the hopes of bringing them back to life—is plastination. Invented in Germany in the 1970s, plastination uses plastic to replace the water and fat in the body parts of cadavers. The resulting body part does not decay and is medically so accurate that it retains most of the microscopic properties of the original. Plastinated body parts are used in some medical schools for anatomy study. The technique is also in use in a popular traveling exhibit about the human body, Body Worlds.

Finding More Mummies

But not all mummy research involves analyzing ancient mummies or creating new ones. There is still plenty of opportunity for

Another modern technique for preserving bodies is plastination. Invented in Germany in the 1970s, plastination uses plastic to replace the water and fat in the body parts of cadavers. The resulting body part does not decay and is medically so accurate that it retains most of the microscopic properties of the original. Plastinated body parts are used in some medical schools for anatomy study. The technique is also in use in a popular traveling exhibit about the human body, Body Worlds.

"**QUOTE**"

"For many years, the only way to extract . . . data from Egyptian mummies was to unwrap them— a process both destructive and irreversible. Then, the advent of modern non-invasive imaging techniques . . . made it possible to look inside a mummy without disturbing the wrappings in any way."

—Archaeologist John H. Taylor.

old-fashioned archaeological field work. In other words, there are still plenty of ancient mummies yet to be found. They may not be on the scale of King Tut, Juanita, or Ötzi, but, Howard Reid writes, "I have little doubt that major finds will continue to come to light . . . over the next few years."[69]

For example, an important discovery was made in Egypt in 1996. A donkey's foot sank through sand and accidentally broke through the roof of a huge tomb. It was found to contain over 100 mummies dating from about A.D. 300.

The new find opened up a vast region, the Valley of the Golden Mummies, now estimated to be about 4 square miles (10 sq. km) in area. It is still being explored and its findings examined. Dr. Zahi Hawass, a leading Egyptologist, estimates that as many as 10,000 mummies, many of them beautifully decorated, may still be hidden there.

And so mummies will continue to fascinate and mystify people for generations to come. These ancient riddles are waiting patiently. Future explorers and scientists will have a chance to find, study, and marvel over them.

NOTES

Introduction: Meet the Mummies

1. Ron Beckett and Jerry Conlogue, *Mummy Dearest: How Two Guys in a Potato Chip Truck Changed the Way the Living See the Dead.* Guilford, CT: Lyons, 2005, p. ix.
2. Heather Pringle, *The Mummy Congress: Science, Obsession, and the Everlasting Dead.* New York: Hyperion/Theia, 2001, p. 20.
3. Johan Reinhard, *The Ice Maiden: Inca Mummies, Mountain Gods, and Sacred Sites in the Andes.* Washington, DC: National Geographic, 2005, p. 341.

Chapter 1: The Most Famous Mummies of All

4. Carol Vogel, "Mummy's Log: Visited Scan God in Land of the Dead," *New York Times*, August 6, 2007.
5. Howard Reid, *In Search of the Immortals: Mummies, Death and the Afterlife.* New York: St. Martin's, 1999, p. 115.
6. Bob Brier, *The Encyclopedia of Mummies.* New York: Facts On File, 1998, p. vii.

7. Reid, *In Search of the Immortals*, p. 129.
8. Beckett and Conlogue, *Mummy Dearest*, p. 32.
9. Brier, *The Encyclopedia of Mummies*, p. 112.
10. Quoted in Bruce Precourt, "The Discoverers, Part I," Discovering Ancient Egypt, University of Wisconsin-Milwaukee. www.uwm. edu.
11. John H. Taylor, *Mummy: The Inside Story.* New York: Abrams, 2004, p. 16.
12. Quoted in Pringle, *The Mummy Congress*, p. 190.
13. Brier, *The Encyclopedia of Mummies*, p. vii.
14. Quoted in Christine El Mahdy, *Tutankhamen: The Life and Death of the Boy-King.* New York: St. Martin's, 1999, p. 129.
15. Quoted in Challiss McDonough, "King Tut's Mummy on Public Display for First Time." *Voice of America News*, November 4, 2007. http://voanews. com.

Chapter 2: Mummies from the Bogs

16. Pringle, *The Mummy Congress*, p. 112.

17. Don Brothwell, *The Bog Man and the Archaeology of People.* Cambridge, MA: Harvard University Press, 1987, p. 100.

18. Reid, *In Search of the Immortals*, p. 82.

19. Brothwell, *The Bog Man and the Archaeology of People*, pp. 42, 44.

20. Reid, *In Search of the Immortals*, p. 80.

21. Quoted in Pringle, *The Mummy Congress*, p. 115.

22. Reid, *In Search of the Immortals*, p. 97.

23. Pringle, *The Mummy Congress*, p. 131.

24. Quoted in Pringle, *The Mummy Congress*, p. 123.

Chapter 3: Mummies from the Crypts

25. Paolo Ventura, "Dressed for Eternity," *Reportage*, December 2000. www.reportage.org.

26. Michael J. Lewis, "Body and Soul." *Commentary*, January 1, 2007. http://elibrary.bigchalk.com.

27. Beckett and Conlogue, *Mummy Dearest*, p. 145.

28. Pringle, *The Mummy Congress*, p. 248.

29. Anneli Rufus, *Magnificent Corpses.* New York: Marlowe, 1999, p. 213.

30. Pringle, *The Mummy Congress*, p. 248.

31. Rufus, *Magnificent Corpses*, p. 3.

32. Joan Carroll Cruz, *The Incorruptibles.* Rockford, IL: Tan, 1977, p. 27.

33. Quoted in Pringle, *The Mummy Congress*, p. 249.

34. Quoted in Pringle, *The Mummy Congress*, p. 258.

35. Cruz, *The Incorruptibles*, p. 128.

36. Pringle, *The Mummy Congress*, p. 320.

Chapter Four: Desert Mummies

37. Quoted in Pringle, *The Mummy Congress*, p. 137.

38. Quoted in Reid, *In Search of the Immortals*, p. 17.

39. Elizabeth Wayland Barber, *The Mummies of Urumchi.* New York: Norton, 1999, p. 20.

40. Quoted in J. P. Mallory and Victor H. Mair, *The Tarim Mummies.* London: Thames & Hudson, 2000, p. 7.

41. Barber, *The Mummies of Urumchi*, p. 207.

42. Barber, *The Mummies of Urumchi*, p. 25.

43. Barber, *The Mummies of Urumchi*, p. 52.

44. Mallory and Mair, *The Tarim Mummies*, p. 181.

45. Reid, *In Search of the Immortals*, p. 24.

46. Reid, *In Search of the Immortals*, p. 195.

47. Quoted in Pringle, *The Mummy Congress*, pp. 298–99.

48. Reid, *In Search of the Immortals*, p. 218.

Chapter 5: Mummies Out in the Cold

49. Quoted in Brenda Fowler, *Iceman: Uncovering the Life and Times of a Prehistoric Man Found in an Alpine*

Glacier. New York: Random House, 2000, p. 19.

50. Quoted in Fowler, *Iceman,* p. 40.
51. Fowler, *Iceman,* p. 152.
52. Christine Gorman, "Return of the Ice Maiden," *Time,* November 6, 1995. www.time.com.
53. Quoted in Reinhard, *The Ice Maiden,* p. 70.
54. Quoted in Reinhard, *The Ice Maiden,* p. 311.
55. Reid, *In Search of the Immortals,* p. 66.
56. Quoted in Jens Peder Hart Hansen, Jorgen Meldgaard, and Jorgen Nordqvist, eds., *The Greenland Mummies.* Washington, DC: Smithsonian Institution, 1991, p. 58.
57. Brier, *The Encyclopedia of Mummies,* pp. 58–60.

Chapter 6: Thoroughly Modern Mummies
58. Pringle, *The Mummy Congress,* p. 280.

59. Quoted in Brier, *The Encyclopedia of Mummies,* p. 94.
60. Quoted in Adam Tanner, "Lucky Stiff—Preservation of Vladimir I. Lenin's Embalmed Corpse," *National Review,* November 7, 1994. http://findarticles.com.
61. Pringle, *The Mummy Congress,* p. 288.
62. Brier, *The Encyclopedia of Mummies,* p. 139.
63. Taylor, *Mummy,* p. 7.
64. Quoted in Mummiesfilm.com, "Q&A, Dr. Bob Brier, PhD (Egyptologist)." www.mummiesfilm.com.
65. Quoted in Pringle, *The Mummy Congress,* p. 18.
66. Pringle, *The Mummy Congress,* p. 9.
67. Quoted in Mummiesfilm.com, "Q&A, Dr. Bob Brier, PhD (Egyptologist)."
68. Brier, *The Encyclopedia of Mummies,* p. 107.
69. Reid, *In Search of the Immortals,* p. 176.

For Further Research

Books

Melvin Berger and Gilda Berger, *Mummies of the Pharaohs: Exploring the Valley of the Kings.* Washington, DC: National Geographic Society, 2001. Beautifully illustrated, this book focuses on King Tut and other famous Egyptian mummies.

Janet Buell, *Ice Maiden of the Andes.* New York: Henry Holt, 1997. A well-written book focusing on Juanita.

Peter Chrisp, *Mummy.* London: DK, 2004. Beautifully illustrated and with many good short pieces of information. Also interfaced with a Web site that provides still more information and illustrations.

James M. Deem, *How to Make a Mummy Talk.* Boston: Houghton Mifflin, 1995. No photos, but good illustrations. Focuses on describing mummies and dispelling myths.

Brenda Z. Guiberson, *Mummy Mysteries: Tales from North America.* New York: Henry Holt, 1998. Illustrated mostly with drawings by the author, this book looks at some of the mysteries associated with mummies of North America.

Kelly Milner Halls, *Mysteries of the Mummy Kids.* Plain City, OH: Darby Creek, 2007. A fascinating look at child mummies from around the world.

Don Lessem, *The Ice Man.* New York: Crown, 1994. Somewhat out of date, but still a good, simply written introduction to Ötzi, the Iceman.

Clare Llewellyn, *The Big Book of Mummies.* Chicago: Peter Bedrick, 2001. A well-illustrated, simply written examination of mummies around the world.

Dorothy Hinshaw Patent, *Secrets of the Ice Man.* New York: Benchmark, 1999. A clearly illustrated and well-written book detailing Ötzi.

Robin Place, *Bodies from the Past.* New York: Thomson Learning, 1995. A simple introduction to some of the better-known varieties of mummies.

James Putnam, *Mummy.* London: Dorling Kindersley, 1993. A well-illustrated book with many short, fascinating details.

Johan Reinhard, *Discovering the Inca Ice Maiden: My Adventures on Ampato.* Washington, DC: National Geographic Society, 1998. An account by the archaeologist who found Juanita, with wonderful photos.

Shelley Tanaka, *Mummies: The Newest, Coolest, and Creepiest from Around the World.* New York: Abrams, 2005. Great graphics.

Video/DVD

Howard Reid and WGBH, *Mysterious Mummies of China.* Boston, CPB: 1998. Part of the NOVA series, this is a fascinating look at the strange mummies of the Taklimakan Desert.

Tuggelin Yourgrau, *Mummies: The Real Story.* Santa Monica, CA: Discovery Channel, 2000. A very entertaining documentary that covers many of the most famous mummies of the world. Narrated by Brendan Fraser, star of the recent fictional *The Mummy* movies.

Web Sites

Bodies of the Bogs (www.archaeology. org/online/features/bog/index.html). An introduction from *Archaeology* magazine to the mysteries of the bog mummies.

Egyptian Museum (www.emuseum. gov.eg). Official site of the Egyptian Museum in Cairo.

The Tollund Man (www.tollundman. dk). This Web site, developed by the museum housing Tollund Man, has information about him and other Danish bog bodies.

The Virtual Mummy (www.uke. uni-hamburg.de/institute/medizinische-informatik/index_ENG_16552.php?). Maintained by the University of Hamburg, this is an interactive site that lets viewers examine mummies via "virtual CT scans."

INDEX

ABOUT THE AUTHOR

Adam Woog has written many books for adults, young readers, and children. He has a special interest in history and biography. Woog lives with his wife and daughter in Seattle, Washington.